THE FUTURE OF FINANCE AFTER COVID

Technology and Trends Disrupting the Post-Pandemic Financial World

Enjoy the Book!
- Jason Schenker

JASON SCHENKER

THE FUTURE OF FINANCE AFTER COVID

Technology and Trends Disrupting the Post-Pandemic Financial World

BY JASON SCHENKER

ISBN: 978-1-946197-99-3 *Paperback*
978-1-946197-65-8 *Ebook*

PRESTIGE
PROFESSIONAL PUBLISHING

For my loving wife, Ashley.

CONTENTS

CONTENTS

PREFACE

LOOKING AHEAD

In July 2019, my book *The Future of Finance is Now* was released. I wrote in that book about the coming future expansions of the Fed's balance sheet, ready-made quantum computing hype locusts, ballooning government debt, and a future breakdown of the U.S. entitlements system.

These risks were clear as crystal, but it seemed likely that they would come to fruition in the decade beyond 2019 rather than in less than 12 months.

But the COVID-19 pandemic and economic shutdown pressure cooked the risks and drivers of these dynamics, accelerating a decade of change in under six months. Now, here we are.

Risks and opportunities that some thought might be coming down the road were already closer than they appeared to be. They are now firmly part of our future, making it essential to revisit the future of finance in light of the tectonic shifts and pressure-cooked time dynamics brought on by COVID-19.

That is the big idea of this book. And it's why the book is titled *The Future of Finance After COVID*.

Tensions, risks, and imbalances were already plentiful before COVID-19. Now, the risks ahead are greater, more numerous, and much riskier for the financial and economic systems we have come to rely on.

There's an old joke about two economists sitting by a campfire. A bear hops out of the woods, and one economist takes off running while the other puts on his running shoes.

The economist who started running away without shoes on says, "You'll never be able to outrun the bear with those on." To which the economist lacing up says, "I don't have to outrun the bear. I just have to outrun you."

And so it is in finance.

Finance professionals are always trying to look around the corner because being able to see just a little bit ahead is where the money is made. It's the reason that financial technology — FinTech — has been a hot topic for years. It is also the reason why the future of finance is such a hotly discussed subject in the wake of COVID-19 and it's why I wrote this book.

Finance is often at the forefront of technological moves because that's where the money is. It's why finance professionals often say "follow the money" when it comes to a trade or investable theme.

Interestingly, the big themes of the decade ahead started years ago, which is why I've been talking about the big three levers of finance change for years.

These include **increased access, reduced costs, and easier use.**

The move to democratize financial tools and markets has increased, with people all over the world having more access to payment systems, private equity, and 24-7 banking than ever before.

And there has been a big push to reduce the costs of financial services across the spectrum of activities — from payments to managed accounts.

It's why the previously standard notion of "2 and 20," which represented the percentages actively managed funds used to receive on assets under management (AUM), is mostly dead.

Finally, in a world driven by UI/UX metrics, finance has become a sector focused on ease of use, where it was previously a field that sometimes overwhelmed customers with its cumbersome nature.

These three levers of change have impacted FinTech and finance at all levels in recent years; their impact has become even more pronounced in the wake of COVID-19. In effect, these levers have been the hallmarks of disruption. Furthermore, these change agents are likely to continue to significantly impact finance in the decade ahead and beyond.

Acknowledgements

This book represents an attempt to share what I have learned in over 16 years of working in finance and in the almost five years, since I began digging into the field of FinTech.

But no book is done completely alone. There is editorial work, file conversion, design, and project management. And those tasks require a team. Along those lines, I want to thank Prestige Economics, The Futurist Institute, and the Prestige Professional Publishing staff for making this book a reality. Additionally, I want to especially thank **Nawfal Patel**, who managed the production of *The Future of Finance After COVID.*

Most importantly, I want to thank my family for supporting me in my education, career, entrepreneurship, and authorship. I am always most grateful for the support of my loving wife, **Ashley Schenker**, and to my wonderful parents, **Janet and Jeffrey Schenker**. My family supports me in countless ways by providing emotional support and editorial feedback.

Every time I write a book, it's a crazy experience that spills over into my family life, so to them and to everyone else who helped me in this process: Thank you!

Finally, thank you for buying this book. I hope you enjoy *The Future of Finance After COVID*!

~ Jason Schenker
August 2020

INTRODUCTION

THE FUTURE OF FINANCE

Everyone I know gets very excited when they start imagining the future of finance. They see things as being so radically different from the past. But that isn't true — even after the COVID-19 pandemic, economic shutdown, and recession.

The names and technology have been changing, but the game is still the same.

Plus ça change, plus c'est la même chose.

In *The Future of Finance After COVID*, I present some data and analysis on changing dynamics in the world of finance. These are couched in the notion that this time is never different, even if the kinds of technologies in place are changing — even if the world has seen major tectonic shifts in the wake of the COVID-19 pandemic, economic shutdown, and associated recession.

Big data is no big deal in finance. Financial institutions have always had lots of data to wrangle with.

So it will be in the future after COVID-19. The difference will be that the volumes of data will be vastly greater.

Some of the first writing in recorded history was in the form of financial records, so it should not be surprising that data, and keeping track of those data and records, will be increasingly critical in the future. This is why **blockchain technology** has major use cases in the field of finance. It's not so much its use for cryptocurrencies that could be its broadest source of appeal, but rather its use as a kind of accounting software used for record keeping that could garner its greatest advocates. Also, it is important to keep in mind that blockchain technology — although still a buzzword in many circles — is actually not that new either. It's over a decade old.

Even **quantum computing**, which is a new kind of computing, isn't necessarily different for finance. After all, financial institutions have been trying to find ways to use technological calculations, analysis, and computational processing power to gain an edge in markets ever since the abacus — or at least since the bucket shops of *Reminiscences of a Stock Operator*.

As for **cybersecurity** challenges, those are part of a long-term trend as well. Look, the thieves of the decade ahead may not ride in on a horse, wear a bandana, and have pearl-handled revolvers. And they may not wear a trenchcoat to conceal a Tommy gun. But you can bet your sweet bippy that they're still out to get the goods — even if the main tool of theft today is a computer and an Internet connection. This will be true in the post-pandemic world.

Just like in the Wild West or the gangster era, financial institutions will struggle to protect assets in their custody and for which they have fiduciary duty. This will become increasingly difficult in a future of remote theft, where an ever-increasing number of potential thieves are able to hide behind layer after layer of digital encryption at great physical distances.

Mobsters and terrorists will also continue to try and find new digital means of engaging in illicit activities. They may no longer be able to use paper bearer bonds, but **cryptocurrencies** are just a digital equivalent. And their use has been seen even during the COVID-19 pandemic. We are likely to see similar dynamics in the future after COVID.

On the political side of things, governments will continue to go further into **debt** by spending more than they generate as revenue. This situation could become increasingly dire, as the world's debt-to-GDP ratio exceeds post-World War II levels, reaching all-time highs. Even communism is likely to make another appearance on the world stage under a new rebranded name of **universal basic income**.

As you can see, a number of new emerging and disruptive technologies and trends impacting the future of finance look similar to ones from time immemorial. In fact, even the latest trends and developments during the COVID-19 pandemic appear to be accelerating. They are poised to impact finance in the decade ahead — and beyond.

That's why this book is titled *The Future of Finance After COVID*.

The Structure of This Book

In order to tackle the most important technology and trend factors in *The Future of Finance After COVID*, I have divided this book into four main sections:

- **Market Trends**
- **Technology Trends**
- **Long-Term Risks**
- **Global Trends**

In the first section, **Market Trends**, I discuss trends in place before the COVID-19 pandemic as well as some of the most important recent dynamics in financial markets during the COVID-19 pandemic. This includes a discussion on how these trends are likely to affect the future of finance in the post-pandemic period. Topics in this section include how technology and finance have often been linked (Chapter 2), the three levers of change for FinTech (Chapter 3), the hunt for yield (Chapter 4), market correlations and interrelated trading (Chapter 5), the push toward alpha capture models over research (Chapter 6), and the phenomenon of hype locusts (Chapter 7).

When I examine **Technology Trends** in the second section of the book, I look at the most critical emerging technologies that were ascending before the COVID-19 pandemic, and which have found increasing appeal during the pandemic, economic shutdown, and recession. These are likely to impact the future of finance for years and decades to come, and include big data (Chapter 8), automation (Chapter 9), blockchain (Chapter 10), quantum computing (Chapter 11), cybersecurity (Chapter 12), robo-advisors (Chapter 13), and biased AI (Chapter 14).

The third section of this book is dedicated to **Long-Term Risks**. This section is the most dire in the book because it includes an examination of U.S. debt and entitlements (Chapter 15) as well as modern monetary theory, the expansion of central bank balance sheets, and the future quantum state of the economy (Chapter 16). I also discuss the rise of universal basic income (Chapter 17), and the clamoring for free money forever in the wake of unprecedented fiscal stimulus during the COVID-19 pandemic, economic shutdown, and recession.

The fourth and final section of *The Future of Finance After COVID* is titled **Global Trends**. This section includes the optimistic look at the beneficial global impacts of FinTech innovations (Chapter 18) as well as the rising importance of ESG and sustainability for companies (Chapter 19) and the importance of trade for the global economy (Chapter 20). This includes an evaluation of the great power competition between the United States and China on what could be the eve of the Second Cold War.

I end *The Future of Finance After COVID* with individual, business, and professional recommendations to approach the current — and future — changes in the field of finance.

Okay, that's enough talk about the future.

Let's get to it!

CHAPTER 1

WHY I WROTE THIS BOOK

With the onset of the COVID-19 pandemic, I began a frenzied spree of content generation that has included the creation of seven books and eight online courses. The reason?

I became an economist to help others better understand, avoid, and counter the downside risks of recession.

In some ways, I was following my own advice. Unable to travel, unable to see clients, and yet knowing there was a need to understand the tumultuous environment during the COVID-19 pandemic prompted me to create content to help my clients, friends, government contacts, and others.

The first book I released following the onset of the COVID-19 pandemic was *The Future After COVID* on 1 April 2020. That book included some dire predictions for the future of finance and a number of other topics. As we have seen the economic devastation spread following the economic shutdown, there is a need for a greater discussion of what's next for the future of finance and the economy in a post-pandemic world.

But my interest and study of the future of finance did not begin with the COVID-19 pandemic, economic shutdown, and recession. Although I have been working professionally as a business economist since 2004, I really first started writing extensively about the future of finance and FinTech in 2016, when I was working on a FinTech certificate at MIT.

On the lecture circuit, I began incorporating FinTech topics into numerous professional speeches in 2016. In fact, I had a number of these speeches professionally recorded and posted on YouTube at www.youtube.com/jasonschenker.

And then there was The Future of Finance course in 2017 for the initial launch of The Futurist Institute's Certified Futurist and Long-Term Analyst™ — FLTA™ — training program.

I also wrote a book in 2019 titled *The Future of Finance is Now* in response to client and agent demands. That book became a bestseller on Amazon, has been licensed overseas, and actually followed a number of books I had previously written about future technology that included sections dedicated to the future of finance, including *Jobs for Robots, The Promise of Blockchain, The Robot and Automation Almanac,* and *Quantum: Computing Nouveau.*

The notion of using a book as a business card has become commonplace. But I myself sometimes forget that no matter how much research I produce, no matter how many speeches I give, and no matter how many articles or videos I create, it very often does not matter.

Plus, if you have not written a book on a certain subject, people simply will not believe you have any real insight or expertise. This is a critical reason I wrote both *The Future of Finance is Now* and The *Future of Finance After COVID*.

The future of finance is an amazing and exciting topic. It is what fundamentally shifted my entire professional career and forced me to pivot from being an economist to becoming a futurist. And FinTech was the primary impetus behind my founding of The Futurist Institute and the creation of the Certified Futurist and Long-Term Analyst™ — FLTA™ — designation. I was even a FinTech startup founder and executive for a short time in 2016.

Fortunately, I shifted my own companies to be future oriented well before the COVID-19 pandemic. But many companies had not been future-forward until they were forced to be. In essence, digital transformation that informed the initial and current business practices of both Prestige Economics and The Futurist Institute has only started to impact many firms in the world of finance. And that impact will continue well into the future after the COVID-19 pandemic has faded somewhat into the background — and the annals of disruptive economics history.

The future of finance will be exciting and disruptive. And the most interesting part is that most of the changes coming in the decade ahead have already started. In fact, most of them started a few years ago — or longer. Finance has always been an industry at the forefront of technology because it provides an edge. After all, an edge in finance, banking, and trading is where the big money is made.

With that in mind, the future of finance after the COVID-19 pandemic is going to be about market adoption, penetration of emerging technologies into new markets, and complete saturation of certain critical technologies.

But it will also be about ramping up bleeding-edge technologies, like quantum computing, as quickly as possible. And the future of finance in all its digital and virtual forms will be increasingly about security.

Most of the trends in the future of finance aren't just trends we've seen in the technology field. They are trends that have always existed in finance.

On the downside, the future of finance will be about various kinds of sustainability. In fact, the future of finance and the global economy will be impacted by the sustainability of ever-rising debt levels, massive recent central bank balance sheet expansions, and the imminent insolvency of entitlements.

In the chapters ahead, I will discuss some of the most important trends that will rapidly become ubiquitous as well as some that face challenges ahead. I will also place these trends and technologies in their current and historical context.

After all, this time is never different. That is most certainly true in finance, and it is likely to be true for the future of finance as well.

CHAPTER 2

TECHNOLOGY AND FINANCE

Finance has always been a field at the forefront of technology. It's because that's where the edge is — that's where the money is.

If you are going to allocate technology to industries with high degrees of ROI, finance should be at the top of the list because the business of money holds the position of the fulcrum when it comes to monetizing information.

Of course, I'm not talking about material nonpublic information or anything like that. I'm talking about performing market analysis, identifying data relationships, exploiting correlations, and using technology to build a better mousetrap. Because a little edge can turn into a lot of money when the business of finance is involved and you're playing with OPM — other people's money.

This is why technologies of the future have been gaining traction in recent years — and saw accelerated interest during the COVID-19 pandemic, economic shutdown, and recession.

In addition to generating alpha — and outright positive returns, many technologies have been accelerating the pace and ease of transactions, reducing costs, and increasing access.

I'll discuss these three levers in the next chapter.

Overall, the most important takeaway for the future of finance and technology is that any valuable new innovations are likely to be adopted more rapidly by finance than by almost any other industry, because finance is likely to be the industry where some of the greatest financial returns can be achieved. Furthermore, even though the trends of the next decade and beyond have already been set in motion for the future of finance, there are likely to be new innovations that pop up.

Looking ahead, financial organizations are likely to take up the mantle more quickly than ever.

It was a lesson that banks learned following the Great Recession, when FinTech was the digital barbarian at the gates, threatening to erode margin.

The banks and traditional financial services firms are finally on board and pushing innovation forward. This is why many big banks started technology accelerators and incubators several years ago. After all, FinTech solutions pose a threat to traditional financial services. From their perspective, if FinTech was going to eat financial services' lunch, then financial services might as well be pushing FinTech forward. As the saying goes, if you aren't at the table, you're on the menu.

Now, as the world moves toward recovery after the COVID-19 pandemic, shutdown, and recession, businesses will be looking to reduce overhead to boost profitability. FinTech solutions will help financial companies reduce their overhead, but they will also provide companies with more attractive offerings as a means to reduce costs in a do-or-die time of existential survival.

Plus, the economic and financial shadow that COVID-19 casts on business planning, strategy, finance, and overhead is likely to last well into the decade ahead — and beyond. This means that the global economic and business backdrop is likely to increasingly support FinTech developments. FinTech is also likely to continue to garner (sometimes begrudging) support from traditional financial services firms that use their accelerators and incubators to foster innovation to stay ahead of other legacy incumbents in financial services.

In short, there is no going back. The trend to adopt FinTech solutions in order to access and provide lower-cost financial services solutions is likely to accelerate. Furthermore, the future of finance *is* FinTech in all of its permutations, which will continue to be driven by three critical levers.

CHAPTER 3

LEVERS OF CHANGE

Financial technology, otherwise known in shorthand as FinTech, is driving innovation and disruption because of three main levers of change.

The first lever is reducing cost. It is pretty straightforward. FinTech solutions have used technology to reduce costs of financial activities in everything from buying and selling stocks to transferring funds and making as well as receiving payments.

Traditional financial services firms have had to compete with, acquire, or otherwise grow competing solutions in order to remain competitive with some of the lower-cost options that FinTech has brought to the world. Most recently, this has resulted in brokerage houses and banks offering financial transactions and trading at no cost.

During the COVID-19 pandemic, the use of free online trading programs like Robinhood experienced a surge in new accounts — by orders of magnitude.[1] People with nothing to do, decided to try their hand at trading.

While there are significant risks for unknowledgeable, inexperienced trading novices, the ease of use and lack of cost as well as financial market volatility turned into a business bonanza. And other trading apps beyond Robinhood saw their demand surge as well.

Of course, cost is only one factor that drives consumer decisions.

The second key lever of FinTech is user experience. While FinTech solutions generally try to reduce costs, they also strive to improve the customer experience. In fact, it's that experience piece that can be even more critical for success. Apps in the FinTech space have prioritized what's called UI/UX, which stands for user interface/user experience. Because when there's a positive experience provided in concert with lower costs, a FinTech solution has a killer strategic combination.

This makes all the sense in the world of course, because if the storefront of the FinTech company is digital, it should make just as powerful and positive an impression as the mammoth Ayn Rand-ish steel and glass financial skyscrapers of the biggest legacy financial companies like Chase Bank, Deutsche Bank, and Goldman Sachs. For most consumers, the size of the skyscraper is not as important as how easy it is to access their assets, move their funds, and direct their accounts.

The third and final lever of FinTech is access. FinTech solutions seek to penetrate new markets and democratize previously limited financial services offerings. Plus, they strive to provide access that can't be had traditionally.

A ubiquitously invoked example of this in recent years has been private equity crowdfunding. Private equity investments had previously been limited to accredited investors with either high levels of income or assets. But due to changes in regulations, they became available for everyone. Although this has been great for the companies raising money, returns in private equity are notoriously difficult to achieve, and losses can be high.

Beyond the overall access to new investments and asset classes that has been lauded for years as a critical pioneering innovation of FinTech, COVID-19 was really where people saw the rubber meet the road. Before the COVID-19 pandemic, access was typified by an increase in access to insurance, banking, or private equity financial services in a way that was previously unavailable to the general public. But it became a very physical differentiating reality during the COVID-19 pandemic shutdown.

After all, even when many physical bank branches were closed, many apps were still operating. This is another reason people turned to trading apps and other FinTech solutions during the COVID-19 pandemic. Since they couldn't get to their banks or physical asset managers, some were forced to find new ways to fill their financial and insurance needs.

In many ways, this development and move to online banking, adoption of financial FinTech solutions, and the opening of new accounts of FinTech apps mirrored "cutting the cord" on cable television that occurred for many people in recent years — and most significantly during the COVID-19 pandemic — as people shifted to increasingly accessing online entertainment portals.

Before the COVID-19 pandemic, digital access to financial services companies had reached some of its greatest penetration for millennials and Generation X. But in the wake of the COVID-19 pandemic, people across generations have been forced to use apps, online banking, trading platforms, and the like. In the decade ahead, I expect that there will be an even bigger push and adoption of FinTech solutions and online financial services for older generations as well. Furthermore, younger generations — like Generation Z — may never know anything other than online financial services and FinTech.

These ongoing trends and successfully applied levers will foster a continued move toward a more fully remote, online, and cloud-based nature of investments, financial activities, and the financial services industry overall long after the COVID-19 recession has ended. People have long been looking for low cost, ease of use, and greater access. Those are all easier to provide at scale online with zero marginal cost applications. Furthermore, as people continue to socially distance and restrict their interactions with the outside world, they may increasingly — and permanently — eschew transactions done in banks, insurance offices, accounting firms, or with the advice of an in-person financial advisor.

I expect that in-person (or semi-in-person) expertise will still be utilized as a bifurcation in financial services likely emerges. Consumers at the highest end of the market will likely pay a premium for that expertise, while the average retail investor struggles to make increasingly complicated financial decisions with little or no guidance.

CHAPTER 4

THE HUNT FOR YIELD

One of the biggest challenges of the past few years has been the hunt for yield — the hunt for investment returns. Bond yields are low, Treasury yields are low, real estate prices are up, and equity multiples are high. With the ever-expanding balance sheets of major central banks in response to the COVID-19 pandemic and economic shutdown, these dynamics have become even more exacerbated.

So, where are people supposed to invest to generate returns? This is a particularly gnawing question — especially if you are looking for stable fixed income investments with relatively safe returns. And this isn't just a U.S. phenomenon. Yields have fallen almost everywhere.

In Europe, the ECB has had negative deposit rates since 2014, and the ECB seems likely to have negative deposit rates for the foreseeable future — especially after the COVID-19 pandemic. Moreover, these kinds of challenges could remain in play for a long time, since the future of finance seems likely to be a future of persistently low interest rates.

This seems especially true if central banks are going to roll out the balance sheets every time there is a downturn in the future, as they have in the wake of the COVID-19 pandemic. I have been expecting this dynamic since 2016, but it isn't the only reason why the hunt for yield has become more challenging.

One of the factors that has been driving yields lower and multiples higher is a greatly reduced number of investible assets.

In fact, the number of publicly traded companies has fallen sharply — by almost half — in recent years, as can be seen in Figure 4-1. Furthermore, the number of publicly traded companies is likely to fall further, especially after COVID-19.

Figure 4-1: Number of Publicly Traded Companies[1]

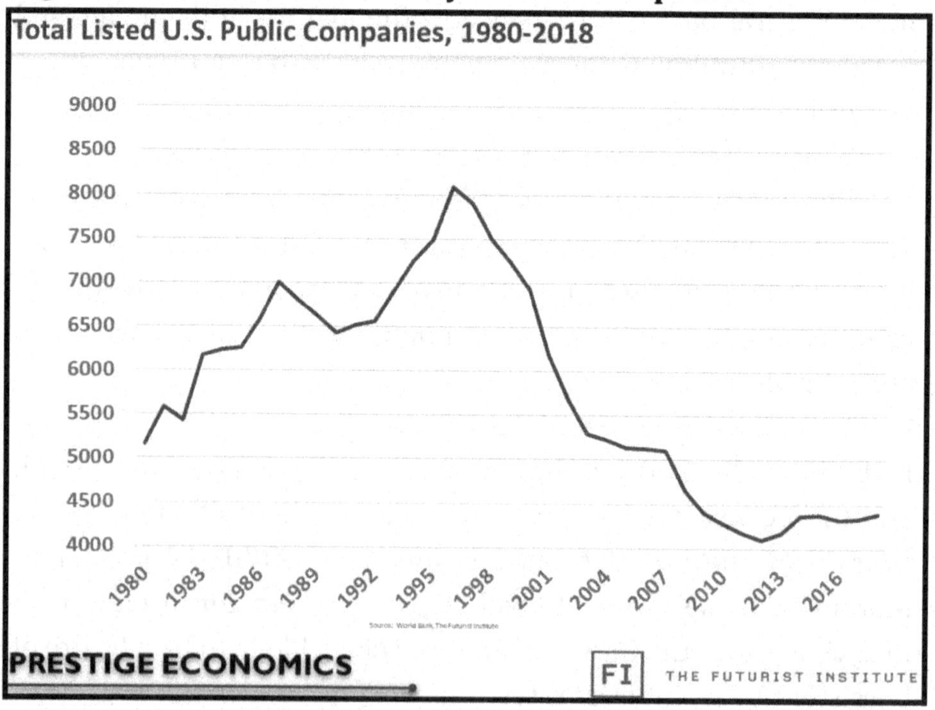

Increased M&A activity could occur following the COVID-19 pandemic, shutdown, and recession for airlines, hotel chains, restaurant chains, automotive manufacturers, oil and gas companies, and many other types of companies looking to spread their overhead across a larger organization that may be subject to reduced demand or downward price pressure for an extended period of time.

This trend of reduced investible equities leaves investors with fewer equity assets to chase. And it threatens to further push valuation multiples to unreasonable levels.

Part of this dynamic is also being exacerbated by the fact that exchange-traded funds (ETFs) have been big buyers of equities. ETFs are a form of passive asset management that I discuss further in Chapter 9, and the growth of ETFs can be seen in Figure 9-2. Because the number of ETFs has risen, there are essentially more buyers of the limited supply of equities.

In addition to a forced concentration of buying and a reduced number of equities in the marketplace due to M&A activity, there has also been a significant slowdown in the number of new publicly-traded companies that have been coming to market.

In fact, there has been a significantly lower number of IPOs for many recent years, keeping the number of total listed public companies at relatively low historical levels. This dynamic can be seen in Figure 4-2.

Continued merger and acquisition (M&A) activity, ETF purchases, and a reduced supply of new companies through IPOs are a set of dynamics that threaten to reduce value opportunities for equity investors in the long run.

As with other topics in this book, these dynamics are not new. Plus, following the COVID-19 pandemic, the pace of M&A activity could actually accelerate as companies take a hatchet to their overhead and try to cut their way to profitability by reducing overhead through mergers.

These dynamics are also highly likely to continue into the future of finance. But that's not even the biggest risk in terms of chasing equity investment returns.

Figure 4-2: Number of IPOs[2]

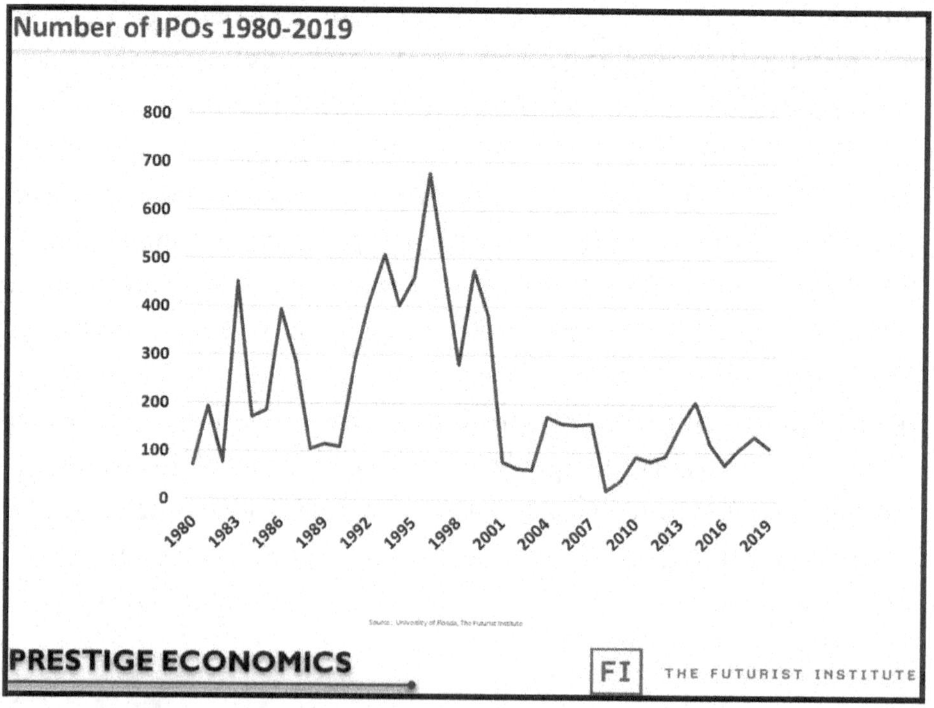

A bigger risk for the future of finance — especially in the near term — is that the percentage of IPOs with negative earnings was at 81 percent in 2018 — a figure that equaled the all-time-high percentage of negative earnings IPOs back in 1999, just before the tech bubble burst.[3]

Historically, there has been a rising trend in IPOs with negative earnings, as you can see in Figure 4-3. But the rising trend of negative earnings IPOs during the most recent business cycle has been more drastic than in previous cycles.

Problematically, this may be a new normal since there are now fewer public companies to invest in.

Figure 4-3: Number of IPOs With Negative Earnings[4]

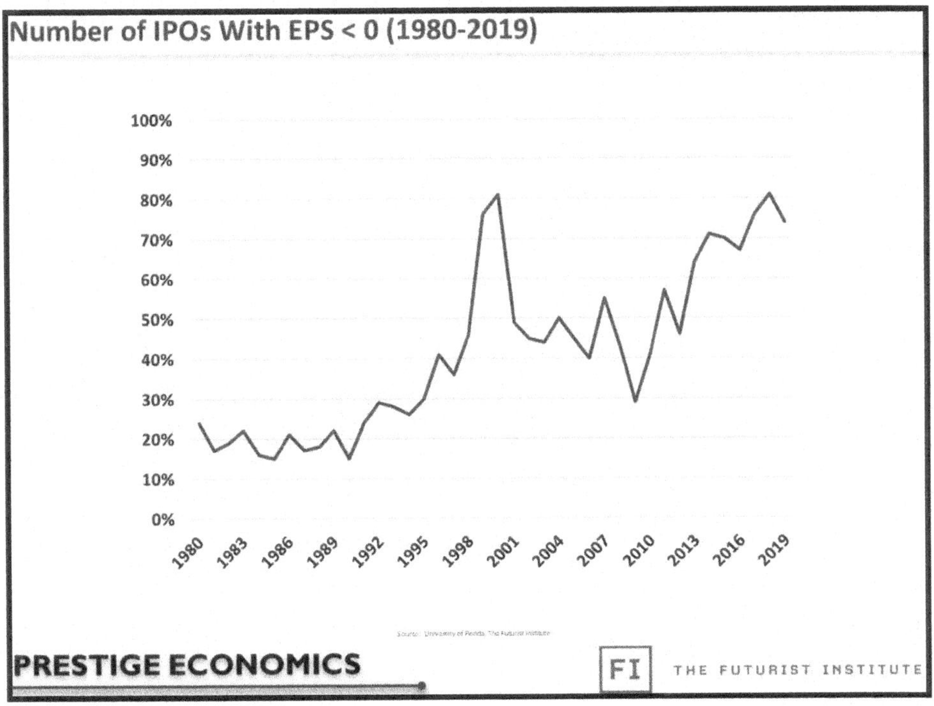

Even if ETFs seek to diversify portfolios, with fewer companies to invest in, that becomes a challenge — and it may be creating additional demand for any kind of assets available, even if they have negative earnings. This may also partially explain why companies that have negative earnings have actually shown greater returns on their IPO days than companies with positive earnings. This dynamic can be seen in Figure 4-4.

Plus, the margin isn't a small one. In 2018, the average ratio of IPO-day returns for negative earnings companies was close to double that of companies with positive earnings. Although that figure fell in 2019, it remained high. Plus, a majority of IPO companies have shown negative earnings prior to IPO every year between 2013 and 2019, as shown in Figure 4-3.[5]

Figure 4-4: Return Ratio of IPOs: Negative / Positive Earnings[6]

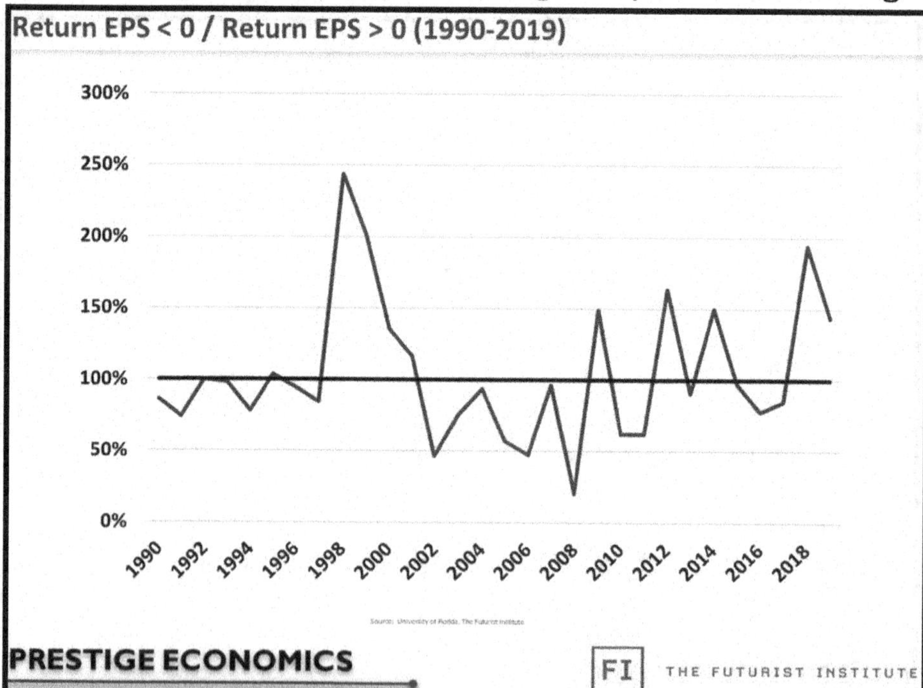

Some analysts and investors typify this surprising and backward dynamic as investing in a "positive return story." In other words, people make investments because the prices have always gone up. This dynamic begins with private funding, where different rounds of funding send valuations of pre-revenue and early-stage companies ever higher. From a seed round to Series A and beyond, all the way until IPO, companies with negative earnings see their valuations rise — despite losing money.

Although the future of finance is likely to continue to see the majority of IPO companies have negative earnings most years, the current percentage is near historic highs — and I have warned that we could be in for a correction in the event of a downturn, like the current COVID-19 recession.

For now, however, investors bemoan the lack of investible assets as the globally-coordinated central bank quantitative easing party continues to introduce excess cash and liquidity into markets lacking a potential for returns.

The result has been a push into assets that may have inflated valuations. Furthermore, the problems of excess liquidity, lack of investible assets, and FOMO have also crept into the private investing space as well. In fact, I have personally seen deals that would boggle the mind of the average person with any basic understanding of business and logic.

Looking at the future of finance, I expect dynamics in public markets could continue to bleed over into private markets.

Additionally, while quantitative easing, which I discuss in Chapter 16, was an effective way to stimulate a global economy on the brink of disaster during the Great Recession and the COVID-19 recession, it has also contributed to excess capital-seeking returns.

The quick moves to enact unprecedented accommodation by the Fed, the ECB, and other central banks helped buoy equity markets during the worst of the COVID-19 pandemic, but it has also made investments generally expensive again. Furthermore, a persistent period of monetary accommodation, coupled with expectations that the Fed and other central banks will always be the buyer of last resort for debt, incentivized some bad behaviors after the Great Recession and the global financial crisis. But it could incentivize even worse behaviors after the COVID-19 pandemic.

Historically, there has been a piper to pay when such dynamics continue for too long. This means that even though equity markets were relatively quick to show a V-shaped recovery in the immediate wake of the COVID-19 economic shutdown, there are still risks ahead. The sustainability of a system that is now perceived to be bulletproof and unable to fail could make the hunt for yield even more challenging in the decade ahead. After all, financial investments offer tradeoffs of return for risks.

But if all assets are now riskless, will assets also be returnless?

CHAPTER 5

MARKET CORRELATIONS

Market correlations have become increasingly linked in recent years and during the COVID-19 shutdown and recession: Industrial metals prices and equities, the dollar and gold prices, bond yields and equities. These prices have been moving around together in the maelstrom of COVID-19 economic dynamics. And these market interdependencies and cross-market correlations are likely to become even more important in the future.

In short, the future of finance will continue to see cross-market correlated price action. The dollar, gold prices, oil prices, metals prices, and equities will continue to see discernable relationships. But these dynamics are not new. In fact, they have underpinned the forecasts I have made at Prestige Economics for more than a decade.

Much of the increasing persistence of market correlations is due to the financialization, algo trading, and technical trading across markets. As more statistical analyses are performed and models are built, trade decisions will likely continue to reinforce historical relationships that may have been less consistent.

Of course, there will also be some critical monetary policy actions and economic data that may continue to exert an outsized fundamentally justified impact across markets. Quantitative easing across central banks, as I noted in the previous chapter, has had an impact of lifting almost all ships, from equities and commodity prices to hard assets. After all, QE programs are designed to juice aggregate demand. And more global demand drives up prices. This was true after the Great Recession and during the COVID-19 economic shutdown.

On the fundamental economic side of the equation, I expect to see a continued market-moving importance for the purchasing manager indices (PMIs) as leading reads on capital-intensive manufacturing industries — and GDP overall. In a not-quite 80/20 world, the U.S. ISM Manufacturing Index, Eurozone Manufacturing PMI, and Chinese Caixin Manufacturing PMI offer insight into the overall health of the global economy, despite the minority of global GDP attributable to manufacturing. In short, these are likely to remain critical reports to watch in the future.

In general, I expect that the fundamentals of leading economic indicators and monetary policy will continue to have impacts across financial markets. And that in between those moments of fundamental action — and in response to them — technical trading and correlations across markets will take the reins. The future of finance for financial market drivers will remain a mix of fundamentals and technicals, while reinforced historical cross-market correlations are likely to become generally tighter over time, effectively removing established and provable arbitrage opportunities across asset classes.

CHAPTER 6

ALPHA CAPTURE

The future of financial market research, like so many other areas of finance, was already at the threshold of reality before the COVID-19 pandemic. And the future for financial market research and trading is called alpha capture.

In Europe, an update to a regulation known as the Markets in Financial Instruments Directive — MiFID II — came into effect at the beginning of 2018 and it required fund managers to unbundle research from the trading and execution components of asset management.

This means that fund managers now have to either pay for research outright themselves, or set up a research payment account with a budget that has been approved by their clients. In other words, institutional investors and funds now have to get approved funds to buy research. That is a tough ask. It has been catastrophic for firms that produce financial market research for institutional investors. Fortunately, my research firm, Prestige Economics, has always focused on corporate clients.

But the institutional and fund part of the research market was very lucrative, and it allowed individual analysts and small firms working with big funds to do very well. Those days appear to be over now.

In recent years, I have seen countless small research firms shutter their operations, and I have seen analysts return to large banks and corporations to serve as content marketers rather than remain independent researchers.

This made all the sense in the world before the COVID-19 pandemic and recession, because the global economy was strong. Financial markets were generally solid and the unemployment rate was at 50-year lows in the United States. But the COVID-19 pandemic upended the economy and financial markets. It also provided incentives for companies to reduce their overhead — and their staffs.

Before COVID-19, I had seen quite insidiously how investment funds wanting to compensate researchers in a post-MiFID II world would engage in something called alpha capture.

In short, alpha capture systems involve regulated, licensed researchers inputting trade recommendations directly into a trading platform run by a fund or institutional investor. If the recommendations turn a profit, the analyst gets paid — and the analyst may even be allocated a larger shadow portfolio to manage. But if the recommendations do not make money, the analyst is out.

As financial firms look to reduce their traditional overhead, alpha capture systems could further gut the traditional asset management field by outsourcing strategic trading decisions to a cohort of analysts and researchers who get paid a fraction of what traditional asset managers would have received.

But wait, there's more.

In some cases, the alpha capture process on the fund side may be somewhat academic. It could be that someone is reviewing the recommendations carefully and then making their own trade, potentially quite unlike what the analyst recommended.

You know, maybe.

But it seems more likely to me that this is a kind of shadow portfolio management done at bargain-basement prices. The systems may take in the recommended trades and there may just be just an "execute" button on the other end of the trade — or there may not even be any button for someone to push at all. It may just be a fully automated system that simply executes trades once an analyst inputs the recommendations.

I had two discussions with funds doing alpha capture in 2018. Both times, the potential for regulatory oversight killed the deals.

In one case, a major multibillion-dollar fund in Europe told me I did not need to be regulated. Fortunately, I had two regulators in my office that week for a review of my Texas Registered Investment Advisor, Prestige Asset Management, LLC.

I asked the Texas regulators directly if the fund was correct, and I noted that I suspected the fund was wrong and that this was a regulated activity. After all, making trade recommendations in a system with very specific inputs, dollar amounts, contracts, and so on seemed more like asset management than writing reports about what markets might do. By the way, that would be true even if it didn't look like I was directly inputting actual trades.

Of course, my intuition was correct. This was a regulated activity. The regulators said so. Explicitly.

When I spoke with the fund the following week, they again assured me that their U.S. compliance department was certain I did not need to be regulated. So I told them what the regulators said. And what would "regulation" in that case mean?

Honestly, all it meant was that I had to share my standard and filed disclosure documents that showed I had a clean professional and criminal background. I was also required to share my maximum fees, although the minimum was set at zero and dependent on performance. In other words, I had to share that if I did not make recommendations that generated positive returns, I would not get paid. That makes sense.

In the end, the fund refused to sign forms that were just a disclosure for their legal benefit. It appeared as if they did not want an analyst that was regulated to participate.

And yet before approving me for their platform, they required me to have a CRD number with FINRA, the U.S. regulator.

In other words, they wanted to ensure I was regulated. But they did not want to sign anything confirming I was regulated or that the activities I was engaging in for the fund were regulated. This means that they probably did not want the regulatory oversight to extend to their platform or activities. Furthermore, I had a similar situation evolve with a second fund.

So, why would you want someone to be regulated if you would then be unwilling to sign something confirming your maximum potential compensation for them — and that you had received legal and regulatory disclosures for your benefit? I mean, why wouldn't the fund want to know that the minimum expense was zero and that I am not a crook?

I have my theories. And I am sure you might have your own now too.

The scary thing is that I know there are a large number of analysts that contribute to these alpha capture systems. And if this is the regulatory policy de rigueur — confirm you are regulated for me, but I won't sign your legally required paperwork from the regulator — then many of those analysts could eventually find themselves in regulatory hot water.

It may also mean that since funds do not want regulatory oversight to extend over into their fund, they may be actively trying to capture trades from those with outsized positive returns. I should also note that these kinds of alpha capture funds may want analysts to sign a disclaimer that the trade recommendations are all legal and based on public information only.

With hundreds of analysts contributing to these platforms and regulatory oversight limited from piercing such funds, I wonder if the goal is to completely obfuscate any trade recommendations informed by material nonpublic information.

Is it all for plausible deniability?

Or is it to keep regulators away from an intentional mix of both modestly positive and very outsized trades? In other words, is it to keep trades mixed together like a goulash, in which you can clearly taste the paprika but can never actually identify exactly where it is?

I know not.

But I wonder.

And as research gets further decoupled from trading and execution at institutional investors in the United States and elsewhere, we could see a further proliferation of alpha capture systems. Some of these may be above board, and some may not.

In either case, independent research is likely to be decimated further. And analysts may have to make Faustian deals with funds using less-than-kosher alpha capture systems to stay afloat.

This is very likely the future of financial market research for those companies that focus on institutional investors and funds — especially after the COVID-19 recession.

Investment management firms will be looking to slash their overhead, cutting everything from office space and equipment expenses to back office and portfolio management activities.

This dynamic is likely to be accompanied by an acceleration and growth in capital aggregation by asset managers, where an entity name and sales people are merely the front end of an operation that pulls money in and allocates it to funds. The capital aggregator gets the money, takes a spread, and then passes it to the funds, which could increasingly deploy alpha capture systems.

The aggregation, coupled by the use of outsourced research and intellectual horsepower by the actual funds, would also reduce costs of the funds that seek to achieve more positive alpha-generating insights at bargain-basement prices, while sometimes skirting the spirit of regulations in place.

In the end, there may still be a lot of financial advisors, funds, and asset management firms, but they may have far fewer people actually managing the money. The money will increasingly be aggregated externally and funneled off to a handful of funds, just as the trade recommendations will be aggregated externally, reducing internal expertise and payroll.

In the end, the funds will only be responsible for the execution of the aggregated trades. Record keeping will be done internally as well, but alpha capture transparency could be sorely lacking.

I hope I'm wrong about all of this. But I doubt it.

CHAPTER 7

HYPE LOCUSTS

Now we need to have a really unpleasant conversation.

About hype locusts.

This is an ever-increasing and all-too-common phenomenon where a technology topic becomes in vogue, and the media, social media, and then broader society extrapolate the emergence of an emerging new technology to assume it will instantly reach scale to solve some major economic or societal global problem.

The assumption is that these problems are effectively solved the very second any kind of technology is invented. And this causes a swarm of mindless attraction. Hence the term *hype locusts.*

As the hype locusts swarm, they can impact financial markets and private company funding rounds and valuations, and they can even impact political discourse and drive policy to impractical places.

But there is immense danger in the foregone overextended teleological assumptions about a technology as deus ex machina that can make resolving a major fundamental global problem into a simple fait accompli.

Fortunately, this is easy to identify using Google Trends data. But unfortunately, this has been occurring across fields.

It is something that can be seen in the hype around electric vehicles, which is a topic I discussed in my book *The Future of Energy*.

And it is also something that happened with Bitcoin in 2017.

The Hype Correlation

In December 2017, as the price of Bitcoin surged, I saw a sign on the side of the road near my house that said "Bitcoin ATM." It was next to a sign for "We buy houses." As the kids say, "Seems legit."

But only ironically, of course.

In fact, the number of scams around Bitcoin and ICOs became a massive problem. In April 2018, the Texas State Securities Board published a scathing report about cryptocurrency scams.[1]

The price surge in Bitcoin pulled in massive interest around ICOs and blockchain. The volume surged on price, as you can see in Figure 7-1, but so did the question on Google, "What is Bitcoin?" You can see the spike in Google searches in Figure 7-2.

Figure 7-1: The Price of Bitcoin[2]

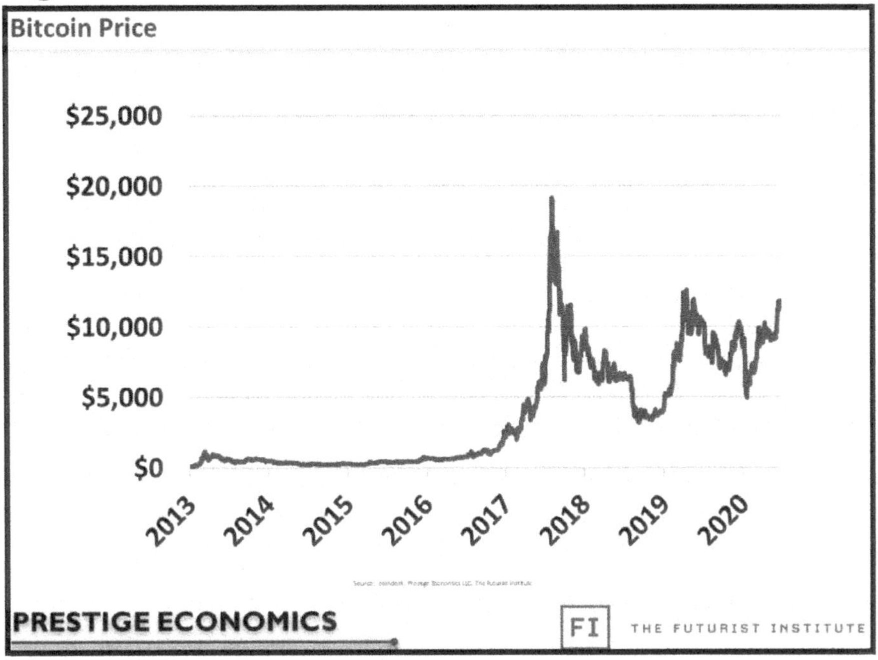

Figure 7-2: Google Trends "What is Bitcoin?"[3]

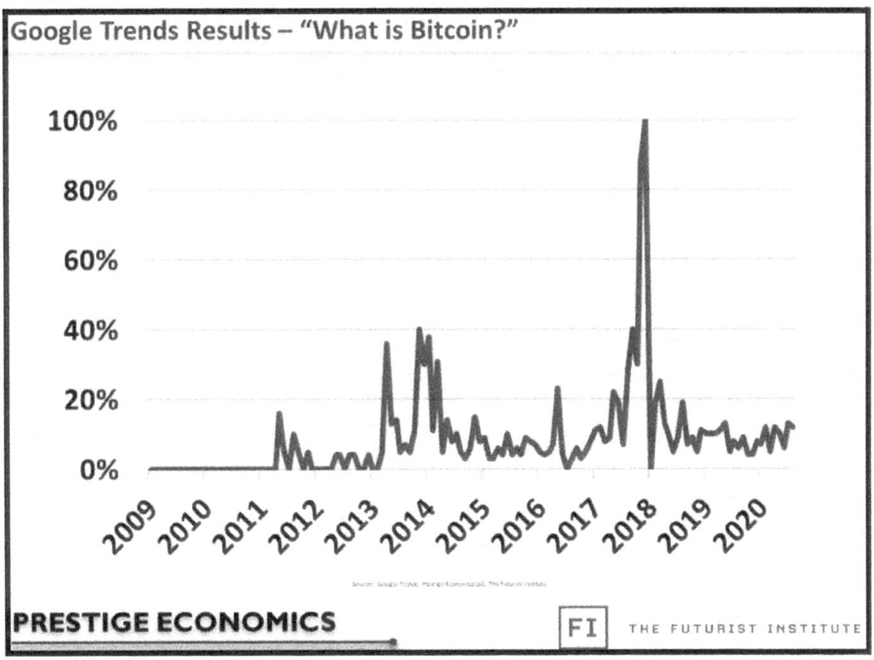

These Google searches indicate the attraction to Bitcoin as an investment by people who did not even know the first thing about it. And dumb money followed lucky money.

And for those companies looking to pull a fast one and rebrand as a blockchain entity, the regulators were watching them too.

In December 2017, near the height of the Bitcoin price bubble, an iced tea company, Long Island Iced Tea Corp., announced a name change to Long Blockchain Corp. This name change caused the company's price to spike from around $2 per share to almost $7 per share. An investigation into the company was subsequently launched, and the price of the company came crashing down to around $0.34 per share as of 1 August 2018.[4]

The Nasdaq also delisted the company, removing it from its public equity exchange, and the U.S. Securities and Exchange Commission subpoenaed the organization on 10 July 2018. This does not seem to bode well for its management, and it should serve as a cautionary tale about trying to ride a bubble, the power of regulators, and the hype around blockchain.

Is Quantum Locust-Ready?

I have repeatedly warned that quantum computing is also at risk of being exposed to the same potential pressures of hype locusts as blockchain. As of July 2019, when my book *The Future of Finance is Now* came out, there were zero publicly traded companies in the quantum computing space. And yet, beginning in September 2018, there was at least one exchange-traded fund (ETF) purporting to be a quantum ETF.

But the problem is that without any publicly traded, purely quantum companies, this could be more of a hype-ready name and label, rather than a basket of quantum investments. Of course, that doesn't mean such an ETF isn't investing in companies working on quantum. In fact, that's one of its core claims. And it also doesn't mean the ETF won't do well. After all, it may do well if the companies it invests in do well. But the existence of a quantum ETF before there were any publicly traded quantum companies alluded to the potential risks ahead for a hype bubble around quantum.

Further recent proof of this risk can be seen in the IPO of QuantumCTek, the share price of which rose by an eye-popping, record-breaking 924% on its first day of trading. With only $7 million in net income in 2019, it's tough to understand how this company achieved a $4.2 billion market capitalization rate on its first day of trading.[5]

For some time, real money has been coming into quantum. And the hype locusts were waiting. I warned a year ago that their frenzy is likely to materialize at some point in the not-too-distant future. Now, here we are, with quantum likely to further benefit from the reductively bullish notion of a megatrend, making it essentially an anointed "sure thing" investment to those exposed to the investment-return-story notions of our current hype-locust-ridden financial Zeitgeist.

But this time is never different. By any other name, these swarms of hype locusts create investment bubbles. And bubbles burst. That, too, will happen in the future of finance after COVID-19.

The Outlook? Bubbles With a Swarm of Hype Locusts

Looking ahead at the future of finance and hype locusts, I expect more hype bubbles that are inspired by content marketing that turns organically or inorganically viral, resulting in a social media maelstrom of hype, which eventually turns into real media coverage — and investor dollars.

This is the dream of every underfunded startup that squeezes its last few dollars raised into marketing for the next round rather than investing funds into a prototype of their actual product. Since the algos follow the data to follow the money, the money often follows the locusts — even if startup funds are somewhat tight in the immediate-term following the COVID-19 recession.

It's not that the world has changed completely. It's rather that the Blue Horseshoe hotline is now in the hands of growth hackers. And the algos that take their cues from social media and earned coverage are just waiting to play the bigger fools.

The mediums are digital as opposed to analog, but the impact is the same as it always was. And the outcome for this kind of investing is likely to end as it has for so many in the past: in tears.

I expect this kind of phenomenon to continue in the decade ahead as the overdemocratization of media and content leads to further false positives in the investing world. It also means that company social media footprints are poised to become increasingly critical parts of marketing strategies — and potentially market valuations.

CHAPTER 8

BIG DATA

The culture of data may finally have been ushered in by the COVID-19 pandemic and economic shutdown. Senior leaders who may have been averse to embracing technology have been forced to cross a Rubicon of technology. And one of the key artifices of the new world will be data.

Back in October 2018, I attended a speech where a Google executive noted that the volume of data collected between 2016 and 2018 was greater than the amount of data created and collected in all previous human history.[1]

Businesses live and breathe data. They are expecting to find their next customers, cut costs, choose their next initiatives, and optimize their activities by analyzing data. But the risk of computational data analysis paralysis is real if the data sets are too unwieldy for the computational powers at our disposal.

Now, after being forced to embrace technology in an even greater way than before the COVID-19 pandemic, it seems likely that data collection, aggregation, and analysis will increase significantly.

If the only solution to processing more data is *more* processors — rather than *better* processors — then the cost to analyze data is going to be an issue that increases with the volume of data. In other words, the cost to buy more processors to get the job done could also go parabolic in the post-pandemic world. And that is becoming a real risk.

In a data-rich field like finance, this could become a critical issue in the decade ahead.

The End of Moore's Law

Part of the reason for the massive shift and increase in data volumes has been a massive decline in the cost of data processing and data storage hardware. But that may be coming to end — especially for processing power costs.

This is because computational powers are facing some potential limitations. In fact, many people working in technology will speak about a big near-term risk, and that's the limit of something called Moore's Law, which is named after Intel founder Gordon Moore. It is the notion that computational powers can be doubled while the costs are halved.[2]

This has made increasing computer processing power technology both more powerful and cheaper. A graphical depiction of the development of computer processing power along the lines of Moore's Law is depicted in Figure 8-1.

But Moore's Law is breaking down.[3] The computational increases with lower costs just aren't happening anymore.

In truth, the only solution now is more processors versus better processors. And this is a really big problem as the amount of data being created accelerates. After all, if you want to be able to analyze data you collect, you need processors that can handle the amount of data you are collecting.

This is going to become more of a challenge as the amount of data we collect and store continues to rise parabolically, especially in an *Internet of Things* — or IoT — world.

Currently, we have an Internet of computers, tablets, and cell phones. Those are the primary devices that have Internet connectivity and through which data can be collected and tasks enacted.

Figure 8-1: Moore's Law[4]

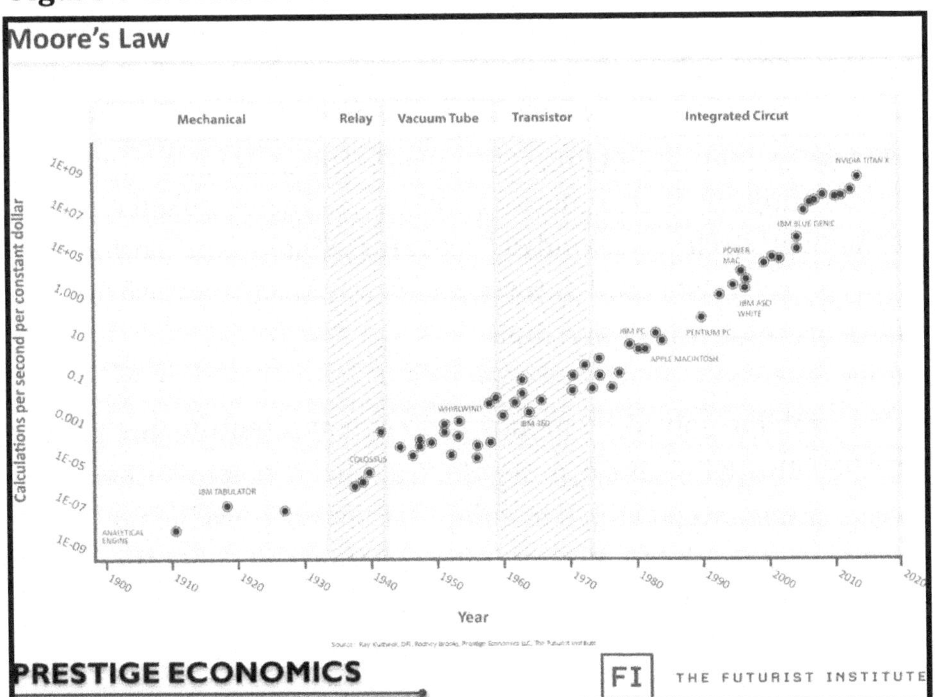

But the drop in sensor costs and a desire for increased consumer convenience is going to usher in the era of the Internet of Things, when many things are connected to the Internet, not just your computer, tablet, or phone. These could include your car, refrigerator, and office supply closet.

Each of these devices will interact, take actions, and generate data. When all devices are connected to the Internet, the amount of additional, minable, analyzable data will be mind blowing. The speed at which this happens is also poised to accelerate as 5G technology proliferates in the years ahead.

Current levels of existing data collection and analysis will likely pale in comparison to future IoT data. And some of that IoT data is likely to be used in financial services, banking, and insurance.

Now, when it comes to processing power, without a step change from technology like quantum computing, the only strategy available would be buying more processors rather than making significantly cheaper or better processors. This is talked about in technology circles as a kind of "brute force" solution.[5] Technology experts, scientists, and futurists use this term because buying more processors isn't inventive.

It's a problem solved by money rather than scientific innovation. It's just throwing more processors at the problem rather than pushing for a step change in computational processing power. Of course, if the volume of data spikes sharply following the forced COVID-19 digital transformation of countless industries, it may be the only way forward in the short term .

Data Challenges Are Different

IoT devices will offer greater access to data in the future than in the present. And hardware may offer the processing power to make analysis more — or less — expensive, depending on whether universal quantum computing gets to commercialization quickly.

But the situation for data analysis is different.

You can throw as much money at the hardware as you like, but that isn't the biggest challenge when it comes to data analysis. Throwing more money and processing at significantly higher volumes of data just isn't enough. It won't help make sure the analysis is good. It won't solve the actual biggest data challenges.

These are some of the reasons that quantum computing, which I discuss in Chapter 11, will become a critical technology as the sheer volume of data we are collecting rises.

In finance circles, the amount of publicly available data is already mind blowing. After all, graphs and charts can be taken from the daily level to the hourly level, the minute level, and even the tic level. In order to develop an edge in trading, you need to be a bit ahead of everyone else.

It's a critical reason why so many high-frequency trading firms in New York are located in Manhattan, so that they can be closest to fiber optic cables that let them execute their trades milliseconds sooner than other firms.[6]

This kind of push for the slimmest of edges, leveraging all of the available data and the swiftest execution, will become more critical in the future — especially since trading has become, and will further become, automated.

Data Balance Sheet Assets and Audits

There is one other final point that needs to be considered about the relationship between data and finance. Some companies currently have line items on their balance sheets for data. The evaluation and consideration of data as a balance sheet asset is likely to increase in the years ahead. This means that data isn't just something that traders will need to have a better handle on. It means that as a resource, more data will have a positive impact on company valuations. And it could mean that data valuations will become a critical question when doing audits of public companies.

The notion that data is a valuable company asset that may be worthy of going on a formal balance sheet has been around for some time, it is likely to prove even more relevant in the future, now that there is a much greater potential for companies to embrace a culture of data following the COVID-19 pandemic — and now that investors are more likely to prioritize the value of data as a critical element for generating future cash flow.

CHAPTER 9

AUTOMATION

Robots are coming for low-skill, low-income, and low-education jobs. But they are also coming for finance jobs too. Back in 2016, I learned that they were coming for mine. If you work in finance, they are probably coming for your job too.

You Might Not Hear the Robots Coming

The first time I heard the word *FinTech*, I was at the Atlanta Federal Reserve Bank's Financial Markets Conference on Amelia Island in May 2016. At this annual meeting, which I have attended close to a dozen times, about 150 of the world's top economists are invited to join regional Fed bank presidents, government regulators, academics, and often the Chairman of the Federal Reserve to discuss the hottest economic, monetary policy, and fiscal policy issues of the day.

Against a backdrop of this prestigious conference, I skipped out of some of the more academic sessions with a Fed reporter I have known for years to enjoy the beautiful early-May Florida weather and go for a swim in the pool.

My friend was with another reporter whose specialty was FinTech. At the time, I had not yet heard of FinTech. So I asked naively, "What's that?" The reporter told me FinTech was "Bitcoin and stuff like that." I knew Bitcoin was a digital currency, so that was that. I didn't think too much of this conversation until several months later, when I tried to hire a salesperson for Prestige Economics. I had difficulty finding candidates.

Highly qualified people were exiting the financial market research space in droves, but I didn't know why. Finally, one senior salesperson told me that everyone was getting out of financial market research because of FinTech. Essentially, robots in the form of automated trading algorithms were disrupting the research business. After being told that FinTech was disrupting my own business, I decided to learn as much as possible about it by taking a FinTech course at MIT. In short, the robots had been coming for me, and I hadn't even known it, so I figured I better get smart on the subject as quickly as possible.

FinTech: Robocalypse Comes to Finance

Asset management has long been dominated by computers, statistical analysis, and programming. And FinTech has been disrupting asset management — often with passive trading strategies. Some of these strategies are known as robo-advising, due to their automated (i.e., robot-like) nature. And the result? Asset managers are losing their jobs, and the disruption potential for asset management is very high (Figure 9-1).

In the movie *Wall Street*, Gordon Gekko asks Bud Fox, "Ever wonder why fund managers can't beat the S&P 500?" Well, with the advent of exchange-traded funds (ETFs), fund managers and retail investors can just buy the S&P (and other indices), which is what they have done. A number of these ETFs are very liquid.

Passive asset management techniques and robo-advising are often easier and cheaper to administer than active asset management. These strategies can be implemented at significantly lower costs than active asset management strategies because they no longer require human asset managers. Plus, there is an economy of scale when computer programs do all the strategy work, analysis, and planning as well as all of the buying and selling of securities.

Figure 9-1: Impact of FinTech on Financial Advice[1]

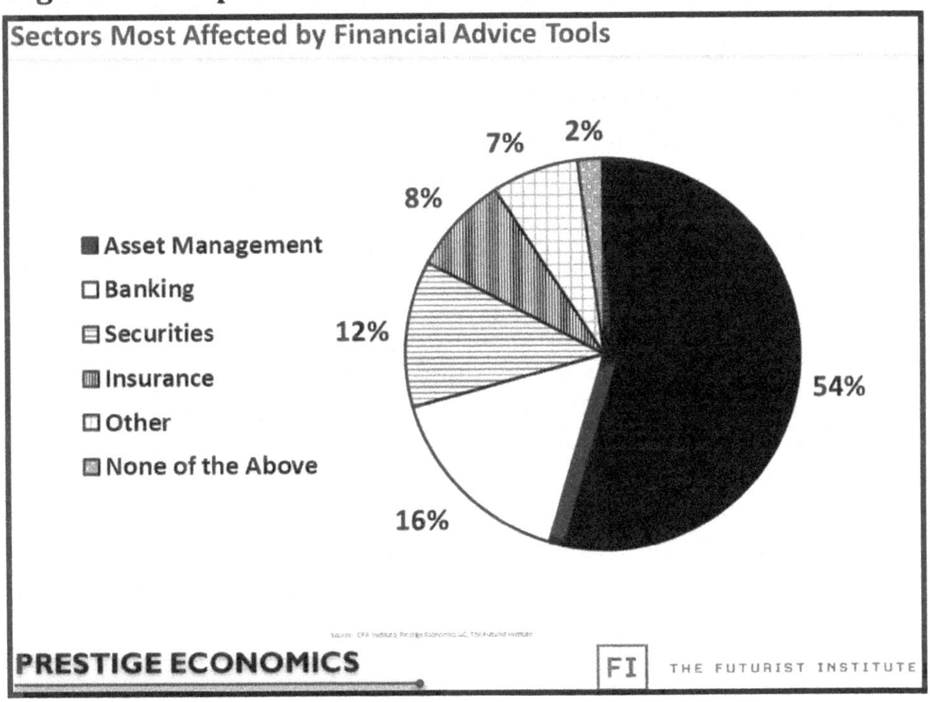

And passive asset management has also been adopted by finance and trading because these fields have historically embraced technology, with many firms using black box, algorithmic, and technical trading strategies for many years.

Expensive items (like market research) would also no longer be part of the budget since decisions are made by computers. After all, trading computer programs do not read words. But they really like lines — especially lines above (or below) which the price of a traded security has consistently stayed for a long time. Technical trading has become more important, so analysts have been trying to add value by knowing what lines and supports matter most for the computers in different markets.

Figure 9-2: Number of ETFs[2]

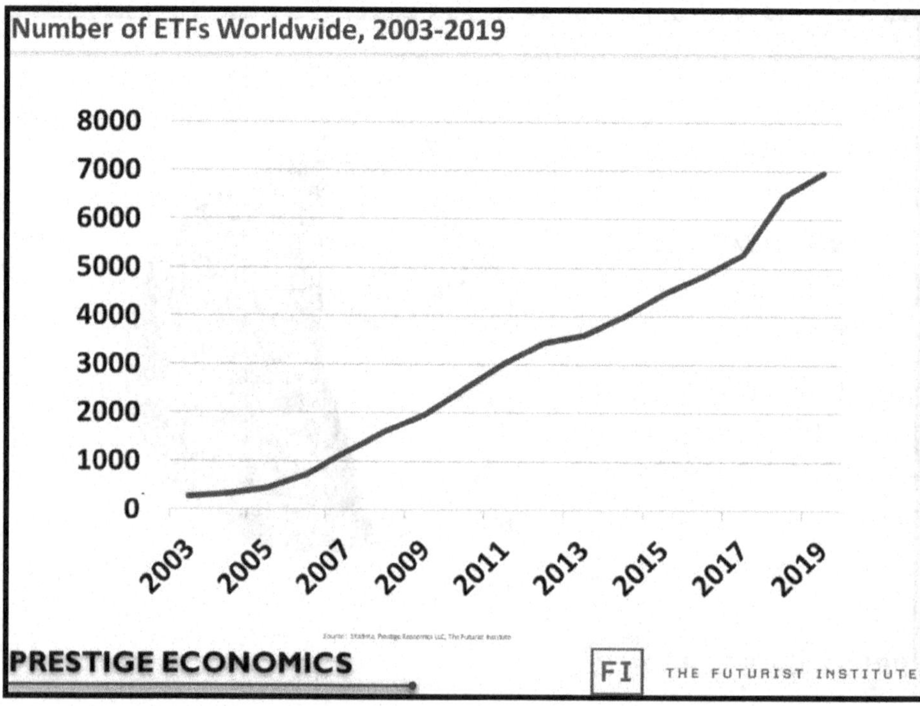

This is why there has been a significant uptick in the number of financial professionals pursuing the Chartered Market Technician® — or CMT® — designation. I received the CMT® in 2016, and it focuses exclusively on these kinds of technical trading dynamics. Essentially, you are looking for the computers in the market. I incorporated these technical trading dynamics into my forecasting long ago, which is why I have long expected that these kinds of trading dynamics will become increasingly important as passive asset management and robo-advising continue to grow.

Everyone Knows

When I first started working on the book *Jobs for Robots* in 2016, I thought I was one of the few people concerned with the issues of automation, robots, and the future of work. And this is a sentiment I have seen held by executives and industry groups to whom I have spoken in the past few years. But the truth is, everyone has been thinking about this — and everyone knows. Not just me. Not just CEOs. Every professional.

Of course, this was true well before the COVID-19 pandemic. Now, however, there is a much broader understanding of automation in the supply chain and of technology, like FinTech apps. Furthermore, with an inability to physically connect with people, the potential for financial services consumers and customers to care whether people or algos are doing the work is likely to fall. This means that everyone from grannies to little kids understands what's happening with technology after COVID-19. Since finance is at the vanguard of most technological innovation, you need to know that finance will never be the same again.

CHAPTER 10

BLOCKCHAIN

Despite its existence for over a decade, when people talk about the future of finance, blockchain is often at the top of the list. The interest in blockchain was fueled greatly by the cryptocurrency bubble in late 2017, which had traders asking, "When moon? When Lambo?"

This mantra can be explained as embodying two questions:
- ***When will the value of my cryptocurrency go to the moon?***
- ***When can I buy a Lamborghini with my modest investment?***

But blockchain is about a lot more than Lambos! And there is a lot of misunderstanding and confusion that surrounds the topic.

Blockchain is like combustion engine. In the way that a combustion engine can be used in any number of different vehicles, blockchain technology can be as well. At its core, blockchain is, in effect, a kind of database with specialized permissions and data sharing that has significant value for corporations and society.

Like many other trends and technologies in this book, blockchain has been around for some time. After all, the first official Bitcoin transaction that was implemented using blockchain technology occurred in January 2009. Plus, databases and recordkeeping have been around for millennia. In fact, some of the first recorded writings are based on transactional records. So it should be no surprise that technological innovations that advance transactional recordkeeping would be important — or that they would be continually improving.

After the moons and the Lambos showed up in 2017, companies parroted their interest in the subject. They generally began to look at blockchain in terms of practical deployment and physical use cases in 2018 and 2019. This means that for the future of finance, considering the deployment and use of blockchain as a technology — and cryptocurrencies for digital payment purposes — will be an evolving process in the decade ahead and beyond.

But it is also unlikely to be a straight line from now to all crypto. This is because cryptocurrency blockchain technology was originally designed to circumvent traditional financial systems and structures as well as AML/KYC financial regulations.

Best in a Distributed Network

There are a few caveats about a blockchain that help elucidate its usefulness and purpose. The first of these is that blockchain works best in a distributed network. In Figure 10-1, you can see what a distributed network looks like. It's when you have a number of different parties engaging in transactions and there is no central organization to the nature of these transactions.

This is like what happens with regionalized businesses or what might happen with how members of a family might spend their income. You have independence of actions and no natural central repository for all records.

Of course, a set of records can be created and shared with a distributed network for any kind of transaction. But this has historically proved clunky. Anyone who's ever been cc'd on an email chain for a major project knows how difficult it can be to keep track of every update. Plus, sometimes the wrong files are updated, and this can lead to errors.

When I worked in management consulting at McKinsey between 2007 and 2009, this was referred to as a version control error. It was a major risk in almost any project or client engagement.

Figure 10-1: Distributed Network

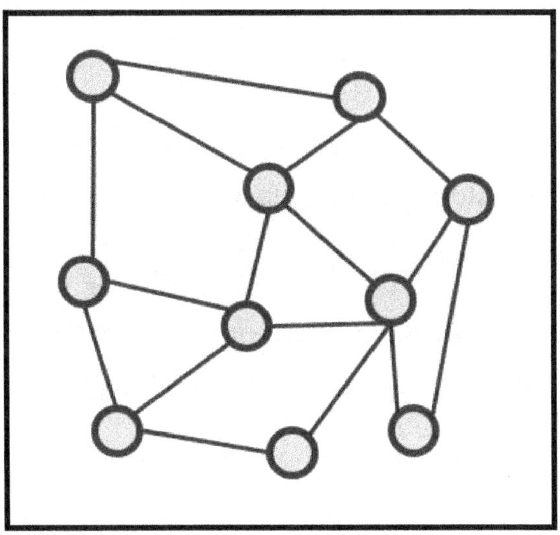

Sometimes people would update the wrong file, and then important documents were at risk of being incomplete or overwritten. And they would subsequently necessitate complicated reconciliation and review. This is also a problem in accounting, which is why for audits, tracking financial documents is critical. For auditors, ensuring a consistency of the data through proper sampling and testing is designed to reveal the kinds of problems that stem from improperly kept records — records that are more prone to errors in distributed networks.

Of course, fixing the risks of record keeping in a distributed network is something that cloud computing was designed to do. In cloud computing technology, people in different locations can edit documents that are updated in a shared location. But those documents are usually kept in a centralized location, and they do not always keep an easy-to-track record of who updated what and when. In some ways, this makes cloud computing like a centralized network, as in Figure 10-2, where all permissions and data are kept in one place. It also means that the network can be vulnerable to a central point of failure.

A central point of failure risk is one in which records are at risk because they are kept in one place — like Dropbox or Google Drive. After all, if Dropbox or Google Drive stop working due to a technology problem, it also means that you may not be able to access your documents. And your system of documentation and record keeping will fail through no fault of your own, at least temporarily.

Blockchain technology is different than cloud computing because it is explicitly designed to allow people within a distributed system to receive updated, permanent ledgers of completed transactions. It is designed to reduce central point of failure risk.

But then there is the whole cryptocurrency piece — and those darn Lambos! But before we talk about crypto, let me just reiterate that blockchain is the technology engine that powers Bitcoin and other cryptocurrencies in a permanent distributed ledger. But blockchain can power many things.

Die Hard Crypto

Maybe it is because the name Satoshi Nakamoto is fake and it sounds Japanese. Maybe it's because people use crypto for faceless, nameless, anonymous transactions that it evokes another fake Japanese-sounding name for me: Nakatomi Plaza.

Figure 10-2: Centralized Network

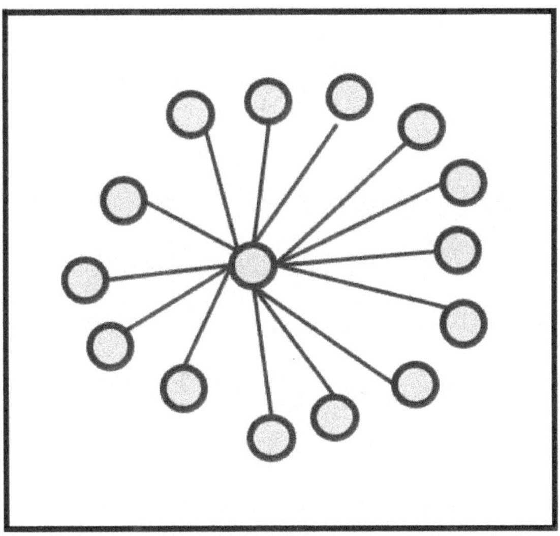

This isn't a real place either.

It's where the first *Die Hard* film takes place — where the villain of the movie, thief-cum-terrorist Hans Gruber, played by Alan Rickman, is trying to steal bearer bonds.

And what are bearer bonds?

Well, that's the really interesting part: Bearer bonds are a kind of bond that no longer exists. They are called bearer bonds because they are owned by the person who bears them.

If you have them in your possession, you own them. If you don't have them in your possession, you don't own them.

You can see a U.S. bearer bond in Figure 10-3.

While bearer bonds were first issued in the United States in the second half of the 19th century, they stopped being issued in 1982.[1] Today, they are all but extinct.

The reason?

Anti-money laundering.

Anti-money laundering, or AML, as most finance people know it, is the set of legal initiatives taken by governments and financial institutions to prevent and hinder terrorists, criminals, and other bad actors from being able to engage in actions by making it difficult to transfer, hide, and otherwise use money.

And how was it that these bonds were so convenient for money laundering? Well, since these bonds were owned by the person who held them (i.e., the bearer), and there was no trading account or electronic or paper record required to redeem them, they could be bought, sold, and traded in an untraceable manner.

This means that bearer bonds can be used for money laundering and all kinds of other nefarious things. It's the reason the villain in the *Die Hard* movie wanted to get them, because they could not be traced, and they could be used for illegal activities.

Figure 10-3: U.S. Government Bearer Bond[2]

Without any record keeping, bearer bonds could be easily used in illegal commerce without concern of detection because you wouldn't need to go into a Chase Bank branch or log into your Fidelity trading account to buy and sell them. You would, quite literally, take a suitcase of money and hand it to a fellow mobster or terrorist who would, in turn, give you the bearer bond.

So why do bearer bonds make me think of the interplay between Bitcoin and *Die Hard*?

That's simple.

Bitcoin and other cryptocurrencies can be used namelessly. Facelessly. Anonymously. They are digital bearer bonds.

Like the analog, physical bearer bonds before them, these digital bearer bonds are only owned by people who have the digital key. And they can be used for nefarious purposes. But while bearer bonds are all but extinct because of AML initiatives, regulation has seriously lagged behind crypto. Bitcoin and cryptocurrencies are ascending, and they have not been outlawed in most countries despite their ease of use to violate AML laws.

The irony of cryptocurrencies, of course, is that the idea of nongovernment currency started as a vision of Austrian economists and free market libertarians. Yet while these same libertarians may praise the freedom of operating a currency outside of government, if their Bitcoin gets stolen, the police and the FBI will surely be their first phone call as a recourse of action.

But it may all be for naught. After all, even though transactions on the ledger are permanent, they are difficult to track down because of the built-in anonymity of cryptocurrencies. And even if improving forensics could help trace ill-gotten crypto leveraging the records of a permanent ledger, stopping transactions as they happen would still be quite impossible.

So, as paragons of economic theory dream of the freedom crypto brings, the Hans Grubers of the world — including ISIS, anarchists, political subversives, organized criminals, and the rest of the digital underworld — rejoice in the ignorance and naiveté of those dreams.

Policymakers Know

Fortunately, policymakers and governments have figured out the potential problems with cryptocurrencies as an anonymous means for bad actors to circumvent regulated structures.

Christine Lagarde, the head of the International Monetary Fund, spoke on the topic of cryptocurrencies at a conference titled Terrorism Financing: The Other War Against Al-Qaida and Daesh.

At that event on 26 April 2018, Lagarde noted:

> **[FinTech] can be used to promote and fund terrorism through the anonymity of crypto-assets.** But leveraged effectively, fintech can also be a powerful tool to fight terrorism and its financing.[3]

The Bank of International Settlements, which is considered the central bank of central banks, noted in June 2018:

> They lack a legal entity or person that can be brought into the regulatory perimeter. **Cryptocurrencies live in their own digital, nationless realm and can largely function in isolation from existing institutional environments or other infrastructure.** Their legal domicile — to the extent they have one — might be offshore, or impossible to establish. As a result, they can be regulated only indirectly.[4]

The big takeaway is that cryptocurrencies exist outside of legal frameworks, and their anonymity facilitates terrorism funding.

This recently became an issue in the wake of the COVID-19 pandemic, when the U.S. government recently seized millions of dollars in cryptocurrencies from over 300 accounts from al-Qaeda and two other terrorist groups that were using social media to attract crypto funds.[5]

For now, the cryptocurrency story has yet to fully play out. There are still many questions that need to be answered for regulators to give approval. And there is no guarantee that their complete approval will ever come. Furthermore, any cryptocurrencies that attempt to circumvent or subvert current, dominant, global finance structures may find themselves on the wrong side of regulation for a long time to come. The murky nature of cryptocurrencies is one of the reasons Facebook's plan to create Libra as its own cryptocurrency was so hotly watched by lawmakers and regulators in 2019.[6]

Assessing the Future Potential of Blockchain

The potential impact of blockchain is bigger than most people can imagine but not nearly as great as some believe. Yet, while many people think blockchain is just crypto, that's only the tip of the iceberg. This was a key part of a talk I gave at SXSW in March 2017, and it was the cornerstone of a book reading I did for *The Promise of Blockchain* at SXSW in March 2019.

The impact on corporate supply chains — on logistics, transport, and freight — is going to be massive. And there are a number of other industries, like finance and agriculture, where a chain of custody of ownership and good record keeping is likely to provide a significant value proposition for blockchain.

After all, blockchain allows for a permanent distributed ledger, and if used in a private, commercial endeavor, it could provide instant transparency of origin, content, and custody, which is often required from a regulatory framework for conflict minerals, chemicals or chemical content, or trade. Plus, this kind of transparency can all have significant value from a public health and safety standpoint, as is the case with agricultural products and food safety — an area that has been at the forefront of blockchain use and adoption.

The potential for blockchain to add economic value in many different industries and corporate fields is massive. But it isn't equal across industries. Plus, in some cases the ROI to deploy blockchain may not be present. In general, it appears as if the biggest value proposition for blockchain is where there are supply chain risks or health and safety issues to mitigate.

Assets in Transition See Greatest Use Case

The value proposition in using blockchains for record keeping on long-lived assets is lower than for assets that move. This is true whether we are talking about financial assets that frequently move between investments, markets, and parties — or assets that physically move. This impacts The Futurist Institute's assessment for blockchain use potential in Figure 10-4.

In addition to movement factors driving the use case and value proposition for blockchain, there are limitations on blockchain's potential uses in some industries due to incumbent regulatory requirements and dominant legal frameworks — especially in the United States. This is why healthcare, property, and government data uses for blockchain may prove more limited.

Figure 10-4: Assessment of Blockchain Potential

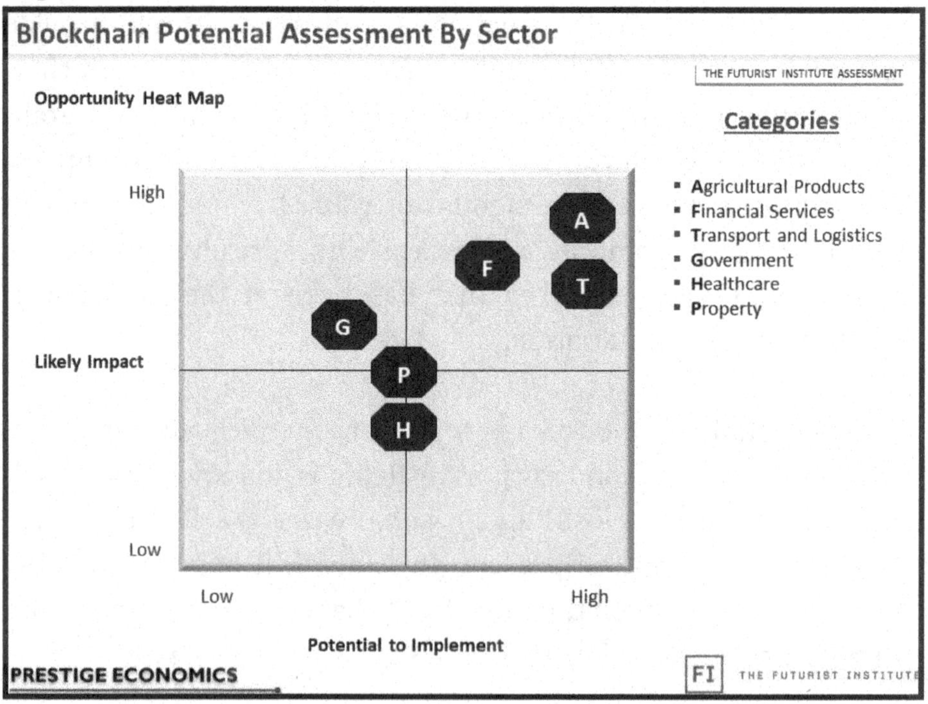

It also explains why there is a high potential for blockchain use in agricultural products, transport and logistics, and financial services.

The Futurist Institute's Financial Services Assessment

As the Chairman of The Futurist Institute, I directed an analysis and study of corporate and commercial opportunities in blockchain across industries. The overview across industries is in Figure 10-4. Additionally, in Figure 10-5, you can see The Futurist Institute's assessment of the potential uses of blockchain in financial services. The areas where we see the most potential and greatest likelihood for blockchain use overall are in the areas of trade finance and B2B payments.

Figure 10-5: Financial Services Blockchain Assessment

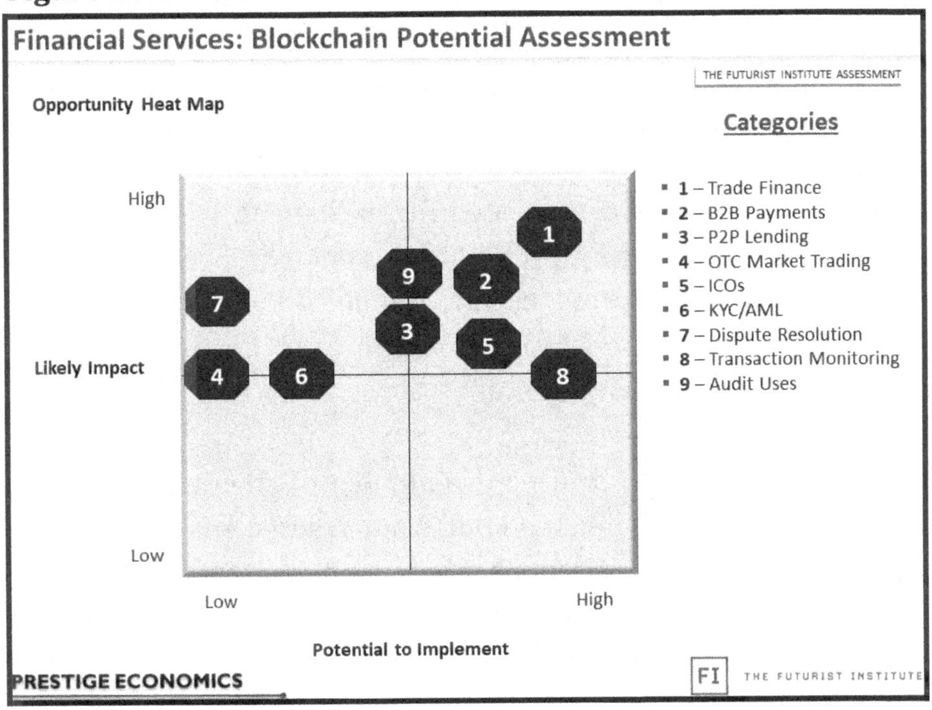

This reflects a focus on corporate transactions as both the highest value and greatest importance from financial record keeping and commercial standpoints. In other words, using blockchains in these areas is likely to bring significant value to large entities — and the economy overall.

From an oversight and regulatory standpoint, I expect a high potential for blockchain implementation in transaction monitoring. This is not, however, something I would identify as a high-value activity for the economy. After all, it is a layer of oversight and regulation but not necessarily something that would likely contribute to the operational ROI of a business. The potential to reduce fraud, however, could generate value.

Areas with a low potential in financial services, in our estimation, are in more complicated financial markets like over-the-counter (OTC) trading. In many cases, annotating and tracking complicated financial structures could prove cumbersome. After all, financial exchanges are very sophisticated, and if these OTC transactions are too complicated for exchanges, it seems likely that they may require a lot of hand cranking, in which case a blockchain may not prove useful. And since these are relatively rare, it may not be very impactful for the financial services industry or the economy overall.

Blockchain is likely to be used in a number of other areas as well. But one topic that might stand out is our assessment of the use of blockchain for ICOs. Although blockchain has been inherently tied to cryptocurrencies as the technology that powers them, the regulatory risk for initial coin offerings presents challenges.

If ICOs can demonstrate an adherence to and compliance with securities laws and oversight, then they may become accepted in the decades ahead. For now, hedge funds and other risk-seeking investors may continue to seek out cryptocurrencies in the hunt for yield. But whether cryptocurrencies of various stripes have a staying power as a viable asset class remains to be seen.

The outlook for crypto is still mixed, even if the outlook for blockchain use in record keeping is much more promising. In some ways, blockchain is a technology that seems custom made for industries with high transaction volumes as well as tracking, regulatory, and safety requirements. This includes finance, transport and logistics, and agriculture. And while blockchain technology is likely to move forward, cryptocurrencies, and Bitcoin in particular, face significant risks.

Hope and Hype

For now, blockchain technology offers the hope and promise of distributed information and knowledge that can reduce costs, add economic value, and prevent a Library of Alexandria-level loss of information and institutional knowledge for corporate, governmental, and private entities. These have been some of the greatest potential contributions that blockchain is likely to make in the years ahead — and they were the focus of my book *The Promise of Blockchain*.

But blockchain is still also seen as hype. It is still seen as Lambos.

After all, it has been tied to the biggest investment bubble in the history of the world.

Plus, when it is used for unregulated cryptocurrency transactions, it could be the fire that threatens to destroy civilization by allowing for terrorists, anarchists, mobsters, and politically subversive entities to thrive.

That is why I see so much promise for blockchain as an emerging disruptive technology. And why I see both the hope and the hype will continue in the future of finance. In the end, regulation and compliance will be key drivers of future adoption of crypto by finance in the United States and other advanced economies. This reality was true before the COVID-19 pandemic, and it appears likely to remain so in its wake.

CHAPTER 11

QUANTUM COMPUTING

Quantum computing is poised to usher in a computational step change in the decade ahead.

Essentially all computers we use today operate on a binary computational model — 1s and 0s. These 1s and 0s form *bits*, which is the portmanteau for a binary digit.

But quantum computing is not just 1s and 0s, which are often seen as allegories for a bit that is either "on" and "off." In a quantum computing world, there are bits with other states of being between 1 and 0, called *qubits*, whereby they can be either on, off, or both on and off at the same time.

As for the impact of quantum computing, adding additional states of being to the computational process may not sound like much, but the exponential impact for computing power is likely to be absolutely massive, which is why it could be important for the future of finance as well as for blockchain and other technologies.

Quantum computing could prove to be a critical technological step change that will materially impact business, science, communications, cybersecurity, and national security. But there are limitations, risks, and challenges ahead for quantum computing to achieve a true level of commercialization viability.

While some industries will benefit from specific new and emerging technologies, quantum computing has the potential to impact a wide range of industries in a general purpose fashion — as has occurred with other kinds of computers.

Like with classical, non-quantum computers, some industries will benefit disproportionately from the use of, and leverage provided by, more advanced computational power. The industries most likely to benefit are those that have massive amounts of data that need to be analyzed.

Because of its data-heavy nature, finance will likely be one of those fields that benefits early and asymmetrically from the ability to use quantum computers to analyze financial markets. This is why quantum computing appears in this book on the future of finance.

But quantum requires both a software and a hardware change. In fact, right now, one of the biggest physical challenge to true quantum computing is temperature, because a true quantum computer needs to operate at near absolute zero temperatures.

That means big physical and material science challenges lie ahead for quantum.

Of course, this doesn't mean that you will someday have a giant quantum computer in your house that is being cooled to near absolute zero temperatures.

But it could mean that you are leveraging that kind of tech in the cloud, as a processor that you access on demand, in a quantum as a service (QaaS) platform framework. This would be like many other kinds of cloud-based technologies and applications.

Of course, there is also the potential that you could have on-site room temperature coprocessors that utilize emulated or photonic quantum computer technologies. But those would still be different from true quantum computing.

For true quantum, we will likely get there because we have to.

In the highest-value use cases, it's critical to remember that quantum is likely to be not just useful — but also necessary. After all, data is being created at a breakneck pace — especially following COVID-19 digital transformations en masse. As data collection increases, more analytics and a better way to break down the meaning of the numbers will be critical.

Changes in data, including creation and collection of more data and so-called Big Data, as well as the need for predictive analytics and artificial intelligence, will be supportive of the application of quantum technologies. And in fact, they may necessitate quantum. This means that quantum computing is likely in the very near future to be not just nice to have, but it could become a conditio sine qua non.

It could in that respect be a core requirement for more expansive and extensive data analysis, especially to solve what I call corporate NP (non-deterministic polynomial time) problems of optimization, efficiency, and outlier identification. And it could help us push toward scientific and medical insights that are just too difficult to see with panel data that stretches the limits of current computational and statistical processing powers.

Of course, we will need to ask the right questions. And we will need to follow a proven and structured data analysis process. If we can do that right, however, quantum could be a gold mine for data research, scientific research, and society at large.

It would also be invaluable for the future of finance.

But quantum is not without its risks for the world. Quantum could present catastrophic risks for blockchain technology, cryptocurrencies, and all kinds of encryption technology.

The highest-potential use case for quantum computing is widely expected to be in breaking encryptions and rendering all current forms of cybersecurity useless. And that means we need to be ready for these widely anticipated threats. But aside from the cybersecurity risks that may impact all businesses, governments, and individuals, most people may not directly notice the changes that quantum computing brings.

In fact, as an individual or small-business person, quantum is likely to be something that proves immensely helpful only after industry-focused software interfaces have been created.

Industries Likely to Benefit

As the Chairman of The Futurist Institute, I directed a 2018 analysis and study of corporate and commercial opportunities in quantum computing across industries. The overview is in Figure 11-1. We identified a number of industries likely to benefit from the computational power promised by quantum computing. Most of these industries deal with large amounts of data.

The industries we have identified include the following: finance, government, transport and logistics (e.g., e-commerce), energy, healthcare, and agriculture. As you can see in Figure 11-1, finance is a field that is likely to be one of the most — if not the very most — affected by quantum computing.

Figure 11-1: Quantum Computing Assessment by Sector

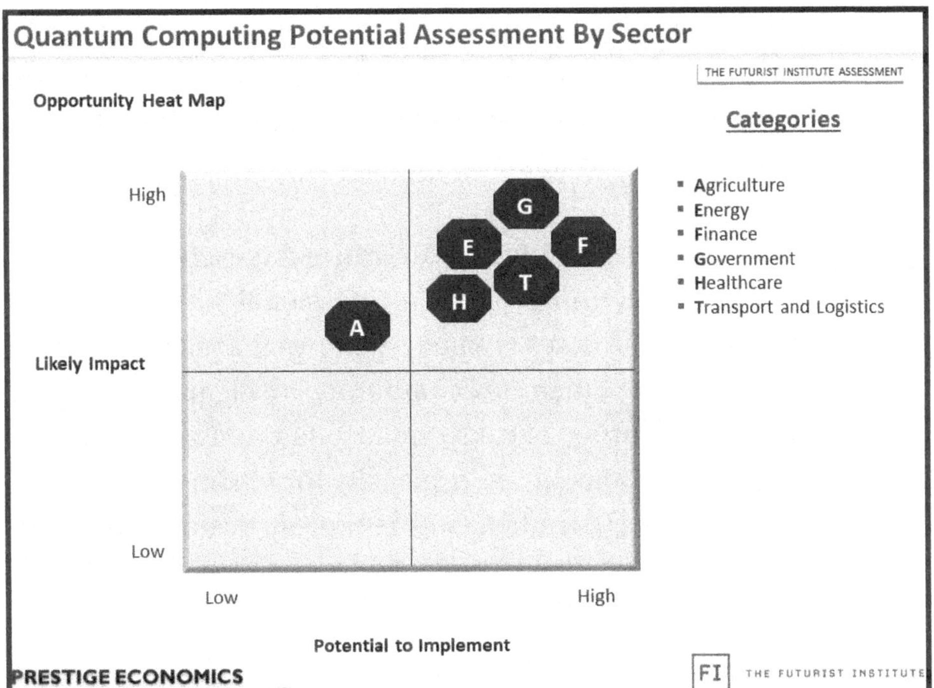

A number of the use cases are purely theoretical as a universal quantum computer with general-purpose applicability and integration with classical computing at a commercial scale does not yet exist.

Also, for the purposes of our analysis, we excluded hard science, engineering, and mathematic use cases even though these could benefit from quantum computing, with massive research and scientific implications. We excluded these from our analysis because they may take longer to impact professionals, businesses, and the economy at large.

For the main industries we considered, we paid close attention to the already-existing use cases for predictive data analytics, machine learning, and artificial intelligence solutions. We concluded that it seemed reasonable that quantum computing could take these efforts to the next level if and when quantum reaches full commercialization. And with quantum, real AI could become a much more attainable technology.

The Futurist Institute's Finance Quantum Assessment

As I noted previously, one of the professional fields with the highest number of use cases is finance, and we have identified 11 finance use cases for quantum computing in Figure 11-2. This should not be a surprise, because finance is often a field that is quick to embrace technology — especially for trading. The rise of algorithmic (or "algo") traders and technical trading has been well documented. Even my financial research firm, Prestige Economics, produces technical analysis that taps into algo trading dynamics.

While data analysis, predictive data analytics, machine learning, and AI are not new, quantum computing could help financial market analysts reach more accurate forecasts more efficiently. This is a massively high-value use case for quantum computing.

After all, if you can have the most optimized — and fastest — trading model in the market, that usually contributes right to the bottom line of a trading firm. And the amount of data that can be looked at in financial markets is almost incomprehensible. Even the best models have some limitations as to the amount of data they can incorporate. But with quantum computing, the volume of data that could be analyzed is likely to be much greater, which could help traders more accurately predict market price action — and reap bigger profits — with **quantum algo trading**.

Figure 11-2: Finance Quantum Computing Potential

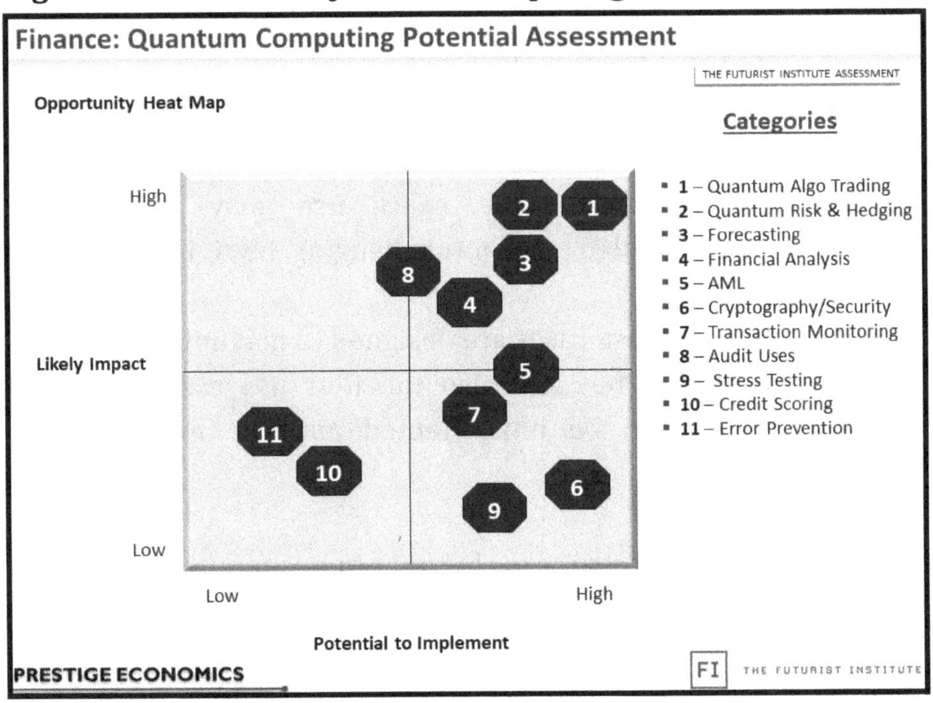

Although this use case may not be of the highest value for society as a whole, it is likely to be a high-value use case for outright financial returns.

Similar to the use case for quantum algo trading — but with a higher societal benefit — would likely be **quantum risk management and hedging** strategies. This would likely involve using the same kind of market data as algo traders but with the purpose of reducing risks — especially for corporations. Firms face all kinds of risks, including interest rate, foreign exchange, and commodity price risks. When these firms miss these risks or get them wrong, it can adversely affect their profit margins. And people can lose their jobs. More effective and comprehensive risk management hedging strategies could help protect corporate profits and protect jobs.

Other related market-based use cases of quantum computing include **forecasting** and **financial analysis**. This could be related to forecasting or analyzing economic indicators, markets, companies, or indices. The exact use may not be as explicit as quantum algo or quantum hedging, but it is related.

In effect, these four use cases are designed to maximize returns in financial markets. They are also the four use cases with the highest potential to be implemented and the highest likely impacts.

The remaining seven use cases for quantum computing in finance are tied to protecting funds, regulatory needs, or otherwise securing the business of finance.

We see a high potential for implementation of (but a lower likely impact or financial return for) quantum in finance for AML (anti-money laundering), transaction monitoring, stress testing, and cryptography.

One use case with mixed potential for implementation, despite a potentially big impact, would be using quantum computing in audits. Accountants may lose their minds with excitement over the endless data that can be recorded on a blockchain, but using quantum in audits may be slower coming — even though it could be a valuable tool in sampling and testing audit processes.

The final two use cases for quantum computing in finance have a relatively lower implementation potential, and they also have potentially lower value as well. These are the use cases for quantum computing in error prevention and credit scoring.

The parallel non-deterministic processes of quantum computing that should help find errors and oddballs, as well as solutions to intractable problems with incomprehensible levels of data, make it an almost ideal fit for finance, from regulation and audit to trading and forecasting.

Threshold of Need

For most companies, near-term investing in quantum computing or installing quantum computers will not be a necessity — even if it were an option. The juice might just not be worth the squeeze, and it might be complete overkill. There is just not a high enough threshold of need.

Plus, for now, there is neither hardware nor software at a commercial level, let alone a very easy-to-use corporate interface or any quantum-reliant apps, that caters to the needs of any specific individuals or industries.

But they will likely come as quantum computing advances. And finance will be one of the fields at the forefront of quantum computing adoption in the decade ahead and beyond.

As with other topics in the future of finance, however, I must continue to underscore that it is important to place technological developments in a historical context. While quantum is likely to be a critical step change in technology, this time is never different.

Quantum computing offers the potential to be a step change in data processing and computational power. And yet quantum computing technology is also at risk from the hype locusts that consume promising technologies in a pump-and-dump investment cycle.

What comes next for quantum computing will be new. But it won't be the new Internet or the new blockchain. Quantum computing will, however, be a new way of computing that will be critical for fields with massive amounts of data, like finance. This is why quantum will become increasingly important for the future of finance after COVID-19 — just as previous forms of computation have been important in past eras of technological disruption and advancement.

CHAPTER 12

CYBERSECURITY

Cybersecurity will be critical for the future post-pandemic world of finance. The threat of a death by 1,000 cuts looms large for companies — especially in finance — that need to constantly swat away cyberattacks. With decreasing technology costs and a potential step change in quantum computing, cybersecurity risks are poised to rise in the years ahead.

The importance of cybersecurity for the future of finance prompted me to complete a certificate in cybersecurity at Carnegie Mellon University in 2018. In this chapter, I share the three most important takeaways for the future of finance.

The first notion is the concept of **resilience**. This means, can your company bounce back? It is a question intrinsically linked at the hip with the notion of survivability. In other words, will your company survive a cyberattack, or will it cease to be a going concern? When I think of resilience, I think of a company that is able to respond quickly to a cyberattack so that it does not interrupt day-to-day operations — or result in lost customers.

The second concept that was put forward in the course was the notion of **resource management**. This is the idea that you cannot do everything you want with the security of a company. This will be one of the biggest challenges for finance companies in the decades to come.

After all, many executives repeatedly tell me that they could spend every dollar of their entire operating budget on cybersecurity and still not feel completely 100 percent comfortable with their risks and exposures. In the end, companies will be forced to make increasingly difficult choices about how to allocate resources for a non-revenue-generating activity like cybersecurity. And this will be doubly as critical in finance.

The third most important cybersecurity concept I took away from the course is **attack surface**, which is the amount of different points and places that an entity is exposed to a potential cyberattack. In any company, there are risks. And with a centralized network, it may be easier to control the flow of information and limit exposures.

Attack Surface and Blockchain Technology

With blockchain technology, the attack surface may actually be larger than with other databases. After all, the system is based on a distributed ledger among many parties. This means that using a system like blockchain to increase security of encryption and transparency of records may have the unintended adverse consequence of increasing a company's attack surface, potentially making it more vulnerable to cyberthreats.

If you work in a company where there's a finance department, it's pretty easy to track down someone in that department if there is a leak of the shipping manifests and payment information. Yes, there is a central point of failure risk, but you have a small attack surface. You know who the few risks are.

But if you start sharing information across a broad, distributed network, there's a lot more risk. There would likely be more individuals with access to the blockchain who could share that sensitive information.

Rising Risks Tied to Quantum Computing

Quantum computing threatens to break blockchains, Bitcoin, and cryptocurrencies. But it also threatens all other kinds of cryptography and encrypted data — everything from your email account to your bank accounts would be vulnerable. After all, decryption is one of the theoretically best and highest-value use cases for a quantum computer because of its ability to perform nondeterministic calculations in parallel.

One likely solution to quantum decryption threats could stem from the theory that there should be a future potential level of unconditional security provided by the use of quantum cryptography due to the same probabilistic nature of a quantum computing encryption system.[1]

In other words, while quantum computing threatens current cryptography and encryption, quantum computing could also be the future solution and replacement that counters those same threats. *La cryptographie est morte. Vive la cryptographie!*

Quantum cryptography dates back to 1984, and the use of quantum key distribution could present a solution to the potential for quantum computing to crack modern cryptography.[2] But despite the tremendous value proposition of quantum encryption, it does not mean that everyone may need immediate access to quantum computers — or a combined regular processor and quantum processor known as a coprocessor. Some users will certainly come before others.

At the top of the upgrade-to-quantum-encryption cybersecurity list are computers that are critical for national security. This is particularly important because of the theoretical ability to use quantum computing to decrypt foreign communications — as well as protect U.S. communications.

Figure 12-1: Chinese Quantum Patents Outpace U.S. Patents[3]

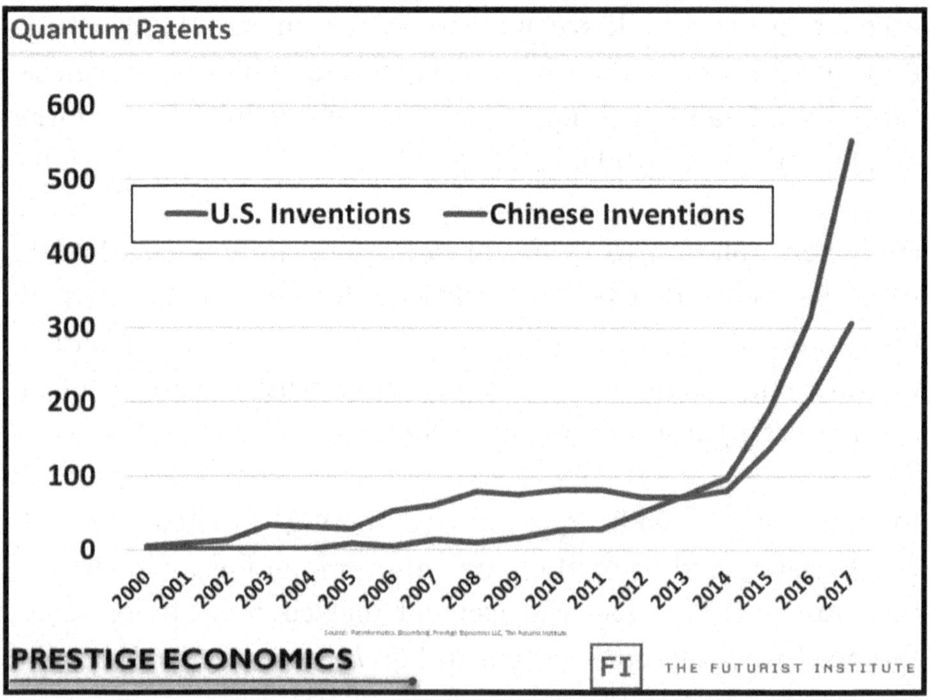

Winning the race to quantum computing is a critical prerequisite for the United States to maintain military supremacy. But the United States is at risk of losing the race to quantum computing, which can be seen in Figure 12-1. Chinese patents in the field of quantum have outpaced U.S. quantum patents significantly.

Quantum physics was one of four major scientific research programs highlighted in China's National Medium- and Long-Term Science and Technology Development Plan Outline (2006-2020). These concerns also appeared in the USTR report that preceded the Section 301 tariffs that the United States placed on China in 2018.[4] Plus, the U.S. Trade Czar, Peter Navarro, has frequently highlighted the risks of losing the technology race with China — including the race to quantum computing. Navarro has voiced these types of concerns in his books, among other places.[5] In short, China could win the race to quantum, which is why the U.S. government has recently allocated billions of dollars for quantum research.

Resilience and Finance

Although national security may be at the top of the list of industries seeking to acquire quantum computing technology, finance is likely to be not too far behind.

After all, if we again consider the concept of *resilience*, it should be clear that companies that suffer massive security breeches could cease to be going concerns. For finance, being able to protect retail and institutional client data and financial accounts is a core fiduciary duty. And banks will be high-value targets in a quantum decryption world.

When I think of resilience, I think of the hope that quantum encryption could make information safer. And financial institutions will see this as an absolutely critical priority.

The push to quantum computers will also likely be particularly high in the United States. As you can see in Figure 12-2, the United States already faces the highest per capita cybersecurity costs in the world — and that's without quantum computers. Plus, as you can see in Figure 12-3, China is the source of almost twice as many cyberattacks as the United States.

These two factors make the U.S. government concerned about a future in which China might win the race to quantum. But it should also make U.S. financial institutions very nervous.

Figure 12-2: Per Capita Cost of Cyberattacks[6]

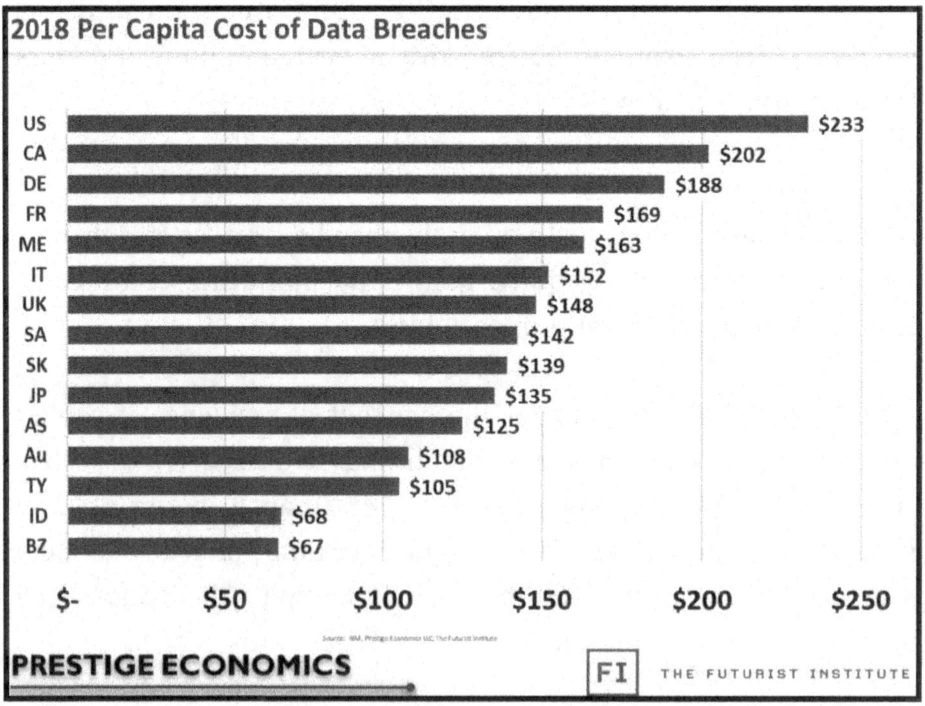

Resource Management and Cybersecurity Strategy

Of course, financial institutions will still need to consider the implications of *resource management*. This is the idea that you cannot do everything you want with the security of a company.

And the same, of course, is true when considering the use of quantum computing for commercial and corporate purposes in terms of time, processing power, and cost. Sometimes the juice is not worth the squeeze — and quantum is not for everything. But it is likely to be critical for finance.

The same is true, of course, with government budgets as well. The amount of resources dedicated to cybersecurity has been increasing, both for governments and as a percent of U.S. GDP.

Figure 12-3: Cyberattack Origins[7]

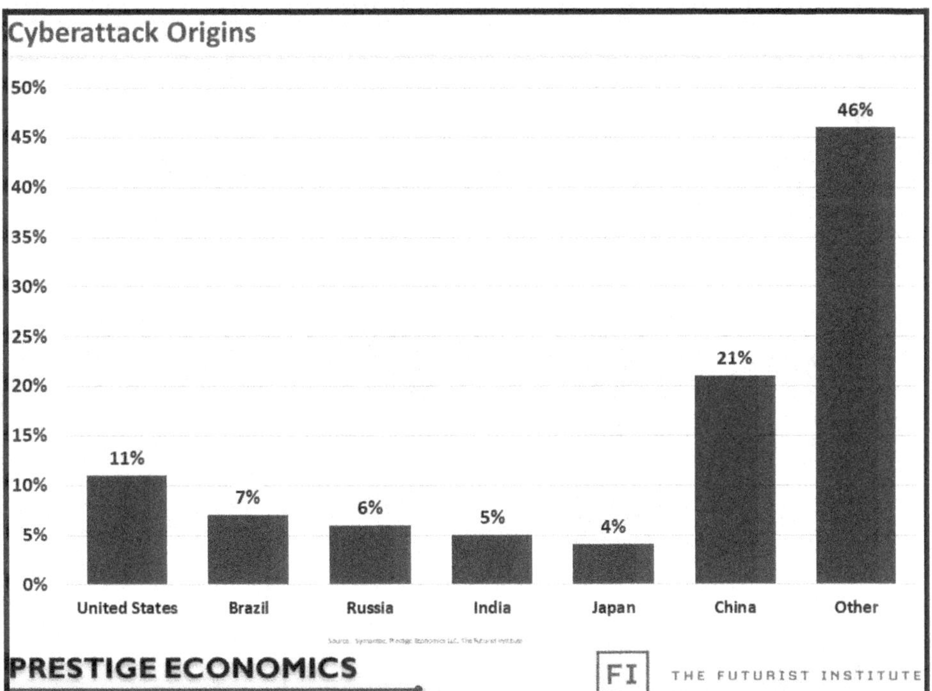

In Figure 12-4, you can see the planned acceleration of U.S. government spending on cybersecurity. And in Figure 12-5, you can see how cybersecurity spending as a percent of U.S. GDP has also been rising. And beyond the national security implications for cybersecurity, it's important to realize that the United States is already dedicating a lot of resources to fending off cyberattacks. And while the United States is concerned about China getting quantum computing first, the European Union is concerned about "potential American dominance" in quantum computing.[8]

It's difficult to really say that quantum computing will trigger a global cybersecurity arms race because there already is a global cybersecurity arms race in play.

Figure 12-4: U.S. Government Spending on Cybersecurity[9]

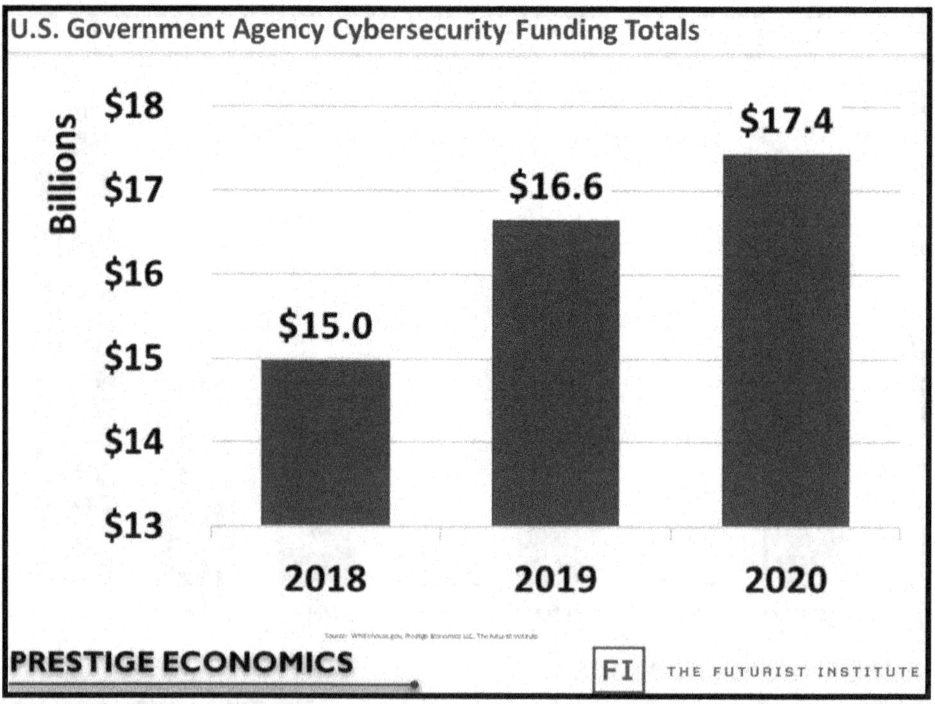

This is why governments as well as companies — especially financial institutions — are spending massive sums and dedicating significant resources on cybersecurity.

Attack Surface

In economic terms, the entire economy is the attack surface when it comes to cyberthreats, and financial institutions are particularly attractive targets. But the current attack surface is protected by encryptions and cybersecurity that are currently effective against most conventional cyberattacks.

But once quantum cyberattacks become a possibility, much of the attack surface could be vulnerable. And the ability to do material damage with quantum cyberattacks will increase exponentially.

Figure 12-5: Cybersecurity Spending as a Percent of GDP[10]

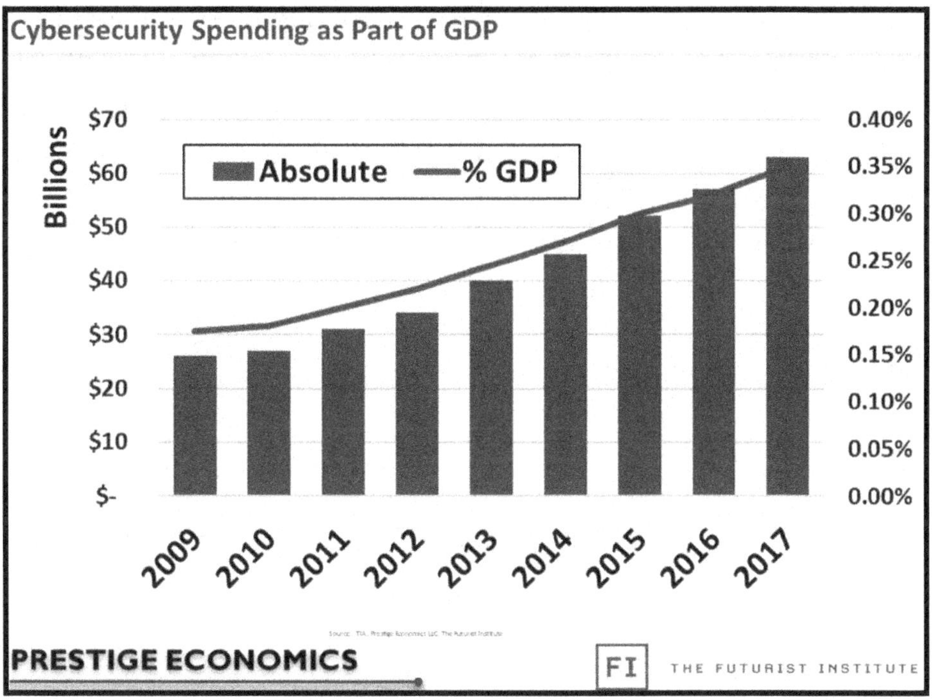

Failure is Not an Option

Corporations — and especially financial institutions — will need to swiftly adopt quantum encryptions to protect themselves from quantum cyberattacks. But these companies must begin preparing for a switch to quantum encryption now — before the step change to quantum cryptography even happens. And if they are caught behind, the impact could be catastrophic.

One science writer for *The New York Times* noted that the difference between quantum computing and classical computing is like the difference between nuclear power and fire. When considering quantum computing as nuclear strength, the stakes become a bit clearer: They couldn't be higher.

Considering the Upside

In early 2019, I gave a speech in New York City to a group of Chief Information Officers (CIOs) from various financial institutions. And I shared with them a number of topics I have discussed in this book. To my surprise, they seemed quite distraught by the information I shared, so I tried to lighten the mood by pointing out how critical CIOs and Chief Information Security Officers — CISOs — will be in the future of finance.

That notion got quite a few laughs. Because it was true.

Someday, finance companies may have very few traders, analysts, and asset managers. But as finance becomes increasingly digital, the importance of CIOs and CISOs will grow. In fact, they are likely to be the professionals with the greatest level of future job security in the entire world of finance — even after COVID-19.

CHAPTER 13

ROBO-ADVISORS

Robo-advising is the catch-all term for automated trading programs that retail investors use to make investments. These robos manage trades, and they are often based on technical, algo, or black box models. Essentially, math and equations underpin their trading. They are another form of passive asset management. But they are also exposed to retail investors. And this might be a problem — especially after the financial market volatility of 2020.

A couple of years ago, one of my colleagues and I called several robo-advisors and we got sales representatives on the phone who were encouraging us to use their platforms. Almost everyone we spoke to had no idea how their particular robo-advisor worked.

If we asked about strategy, the people on the phone did not know the difference between a long fund and a long-short fund. Furthermore, some people we spoke to conflated the notion of a goal fund (what people in financial services usually call a target fund) and a gold fund.

Even in late 2017, I had a conversation with someone from FINRA who told me that despite the almost persistent rise in U.S. equities during that year, the number of complaints and lawsuits against robo-advisors was rising. This begs the question: What will happen following the COVID-19 downturn?

People lost trust in financial institutions during the Great Recession of 2007-2009, and they turned to technology rather than people. But they have clearly placed too much faith in technology. After all, the people who interface with customers, in my own personal experience, may lack some of the most fundamental knowledge to effectively fulfill the fiduciary duty of a financial planner or advisor.

In the longer run, digital market access will likely proliferate and expand in a way that gives individuals a lot more control — and liability — for their own decisions. But that puts all the risk in the hands of potential novices, without any guardrails or guidance.

This means that the future of finance for robo-advising is likely to have a moment of tears. In any downturn, fortunes are made — and fortunes are lost. So it appears to be in the wake of the COVID-19 shutdown and recession. The result? There are likely to be some hefty class action lawsuits ahead.

The recent COVID-19 downturn is likely to show something that institutional investors have long known: Not all funds or advisors are equal. Those that come out on top in a downturn could come to dominate the now still-fragmented robo-advisor marketplace.

CHAPTER 14

BIASED AI

There is a not-small group of market observers out in the world who expect something called the Robocalypse.

These would-be prophets dismally predict that computers will run amok, destroying the world and all the people in it. This is the well from which every Robocalypse film springs (e.g., *The Terminator*). And while there is some reason to be concerned, Robocalypse claims are extreme.

Unfortunately, we need look no further than the miserable failure of Microsoft's attempt to expose its artificial intelligence (AI) pet project, Tay, to the world via Twitter. In less than a day, Tay had learned some very bad things like racism, rabid anti-Semitism, and other forms of unfiltered hate.[1]

Naturally, the project was shut down quickly. At the time, which was several years ago now, I noted that I expected it would be some time before anyone lets its AI project out in public again. We haven't seen another such project from Microsoft since.

The risk that computers will run amok is a problem that highlights the increasingly important need for project management — and oversight for anything that looks even remotely like an independently functioning computer program.

While the prospects of a computer program becoming murderous toward humanity or taking on the mantle of a digital Nazi are less of a concern in the field of finance, the need to monitor technical and algo trading platforms is — and will be — critical for the future of finance.

Furthermore, from a legal standpoint, the use of AI in financial institutions is likely to occur within highly regulated environments to ensure that historical biases, which may have been ingrained in past systems and data by individuals operating with now illegal biases, are not perpetuated further in the present and future.

Imagine a lending institution using an AI program that was making individual mortgage and lending calculations based on historical data that was informed by redlining and institutional racism.

Essentially, that financial institution would be perpetuating those policies by using data from that era. In a way, dirty data could very well have tainted the models that informed the machine learning and predictive analytics that became foundational for the AI created by that financial institution.

Furthermore, that institution could find itself on the other end of a civil rights lawsuit. Even though no individual person may have intentionally made a judgement that supported redlining or any other racist policies, the computer program may have used such data and reinforced such policies in its decision making.

Make no mistake, lawsuits around AI decisions will happen in coming years and decades, and they will become a risk to institutions in the future of finance.

I also expect these kinds of lawsuits could occur in financial institutions as well as many other organizations where AI programs are used. And these kinds of suits could impact a wide swath of operational and administrative areas, from lending decisions and business practices to vendor selection and human resources.

As of the writing of this book, the European Union had already taken big steps to prevent issues with AI programs that could effectively limit their use in future lending and finance decisions.

As you can see, even though the future of finance will include more automation, it could also include additional legal risks. This means that financial institutions will have to do internal cost-benefit analyses to see if AI programs will actually save them money and have a big enough value impact to justify a greater risk of legal exposure.

CHAPTER 15

DEBT AND ENTITLEMENTS

In the wake of the COVID-19 pandemic, economic shutdown, and recession, the global economy has been kept afloat by a mix of monetary policy and fiscal policy stimulus. While monetary policy is set by central banks that have been enacting policies to depress interest rates, fiscal policy has been driven by governments issuing record levels of debt.

The National Debt

U.S. federal debt has been a growing problem for some time. Now, the impact of COVID-19 threatens to make the situation drastically worse. The official federal debt figure from the U.S. Department of the Treasury at the end of Q1 2020 was $23.2 trillion.

But the impact of COVID-19 stimulus measures as well as the additional unemployment benefits to cover the more than 55.3 million people who became unemployed in the 20 weeks through 1 August 2020 has pushed the national debt several trillion dollars higher in just the past quarter. In fact, the national debt is likely to have ended Q2 2020 between $26.5 and $27.0 trillion.

That is a lot of debt!

As you can see in Figure 15-1, the pace at which the U.S. national debt is rising has accelerated in recent years. It took 205 years for the U.S. national debt to exceed $1 trillion, which happened in October 1981. But it then took less than five years for the national debt to double to $2 trillion in April 1986.[1]

Put another way, while it took 205 years for the national debt to exceed $1 trillion, that's roughly how much it grew during each month of the second quarter in 2020. And there is likely to be a lot more debt to come to revive the U.S. economy from the worst labor conditions in its history.

Figure 15-1: U.S. Debt[2]

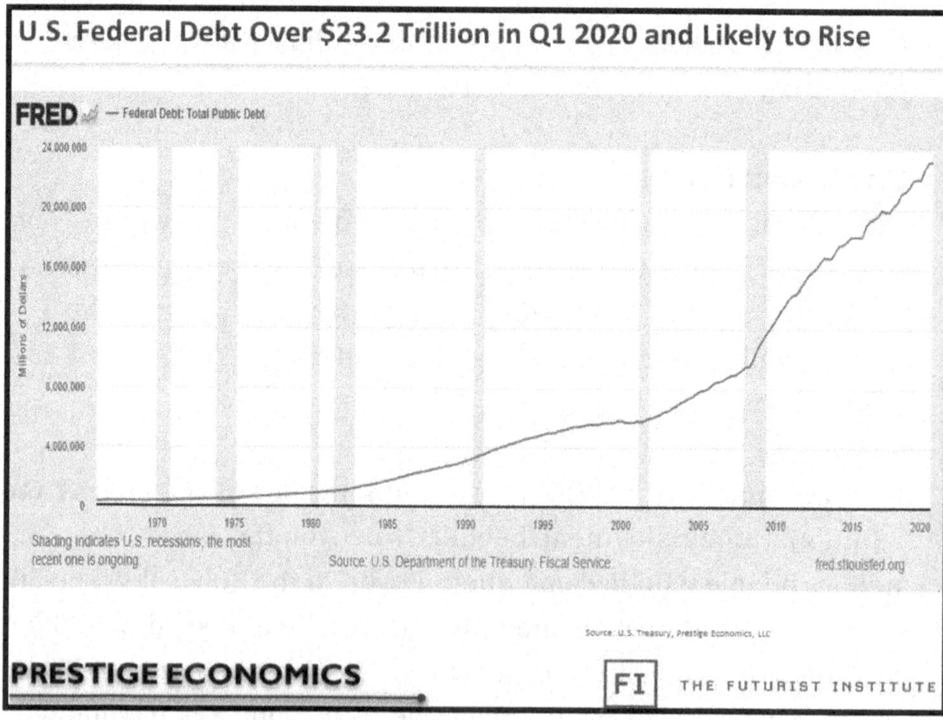

Although not as pronounced as the trend in federal government debt, the U.S. debt-to-GDP ratio has risen sharply since the onset of the Great Recession as well (Figure 15-2). One major negative impact of a high national debt is the drag on potential future U.S. economic growth as measured by gross domestic product — or GDP. Plus, debt exposures can be exacerbated by compounding interest on already outstanding government debt.

Although some analysts are quick to note that our debt-to-GDP ratio is lower than other countries, it is also important to note that the U.S. economy is the largest in the world. This means that rising U.S. debt levels could make it more difficult for the global economy to absorb U.S. debt issuances over time.

Figure 15-2: U.S. Debt to GDP[3]

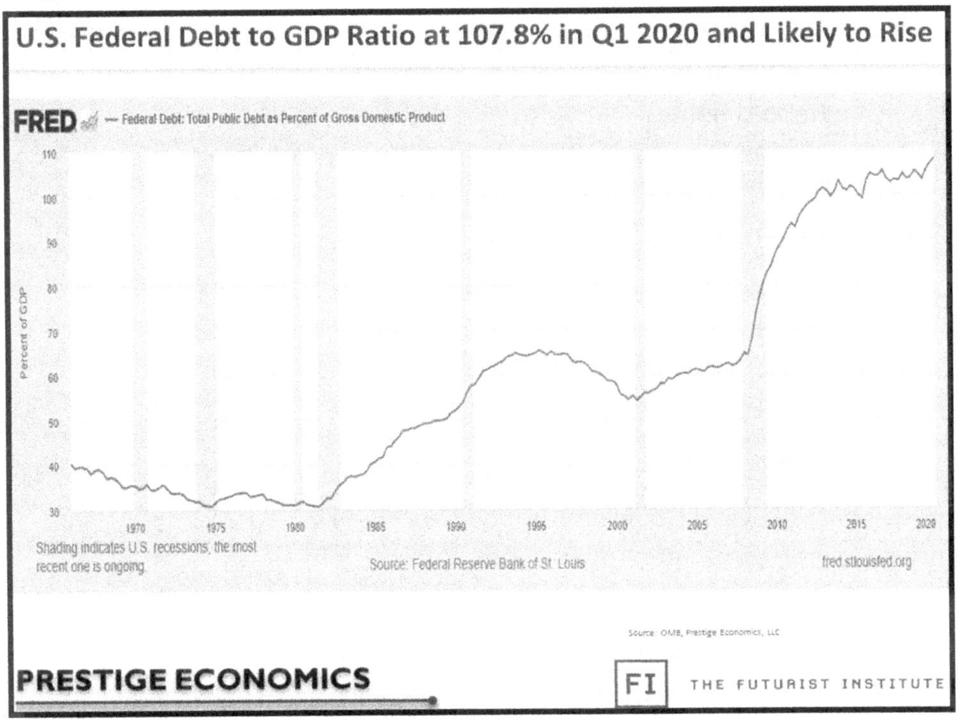

But hey! At least we're not alone. In fact, according to IMF data released in June 2020, the entire global economy has binged on debt in order to survive the current pandemic and recession.

Now, both advanced economies and emerging market economies have seen the highest debt-to-GDP levels since the Second World War — or higher.[4] And these debt-to-GDP ratios are poised to rise even further, as noted in Figure 15-3.

But that's not even the worst news. The worst news is that we don't know how much more debt it will take to get the global economy back on its feet. And then there are entitlements, which are another part of the cost equation that is unsustainable.

Figure 15-3: Global Debt to GDP[5]

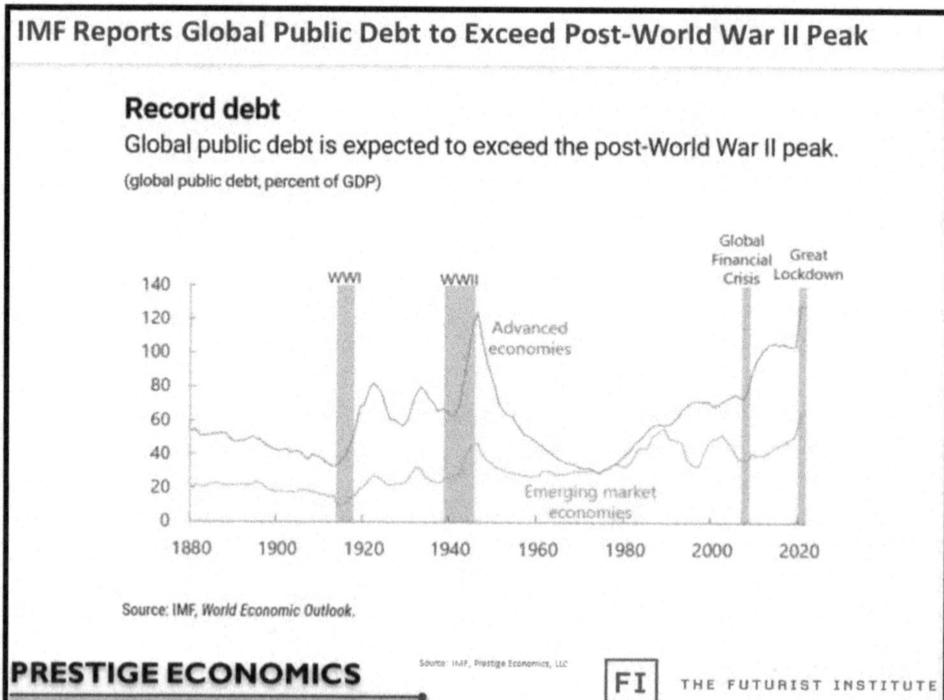

A few years ago, the unfunded obligations for Medicare, Medicaid, and Social Security were estimated to be $200 trillion.[6] And U.S. entitlements have been underfunded for years. This means that the expenses to pay for entitlements have already been drawing partially on the operating budget of the U.S. government.

Plus, this is also a problem that cannot be easily remedied. Many Americans rely on Social Security for a large percentage of their incomes. In fact, as of 2015, 34 percent of retirees relied on Social Security for 90 percent or more of their income. In addition to this shocking number, in Figure 15-4 you can also see that an outright majority of all beneficiaries rely on Social Security for 50 percent or more of their incomes.

Figure 15-4: Social Security Reliance[7]

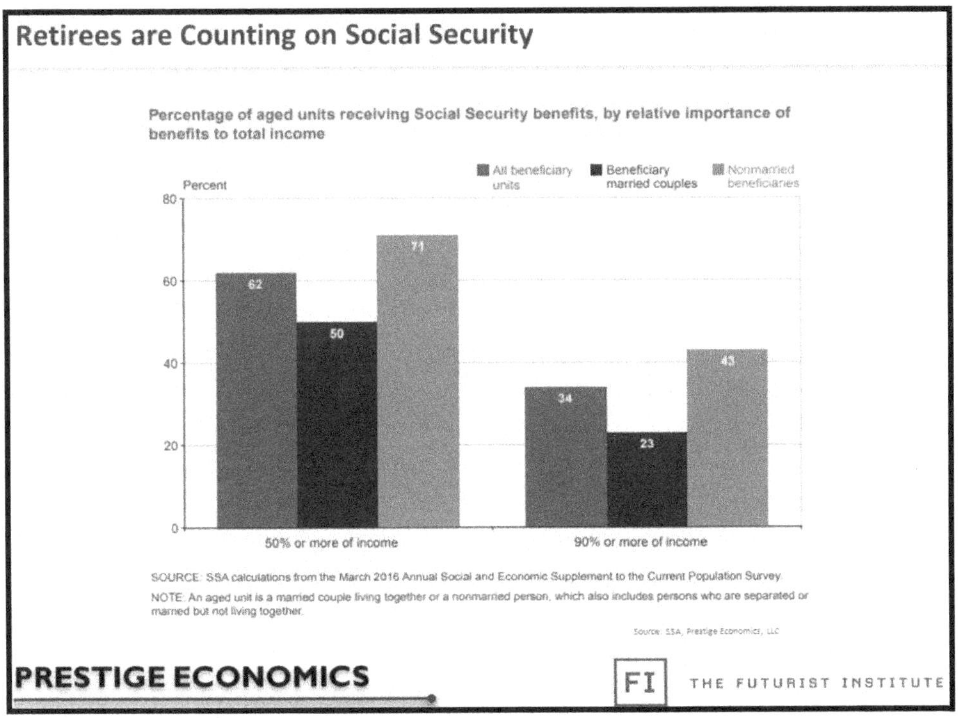

Then there's also the demographic issue that baby boomers have been retiring *en masse* in recent years. This has contributed to a sharp rise in the number of new Social Security awards to retired workers, which you can see in Figure 15-5. In fact, the number of new annual awards for retired workers has doubled in the past 25 years, with the most recent year (2019) showing over 3 million new Social Security awards issued to retired workers.

This graying of the American economy is something that contributes to the risks associated with the sustainability of the U.S. Social Security and entitlements systems. In fact, according to the report issued this month (July 2020) by the Social Security Administration, insolvency lies ahead.[8]

Figure 15-5: Social Security Retirement Workers Rising[9]

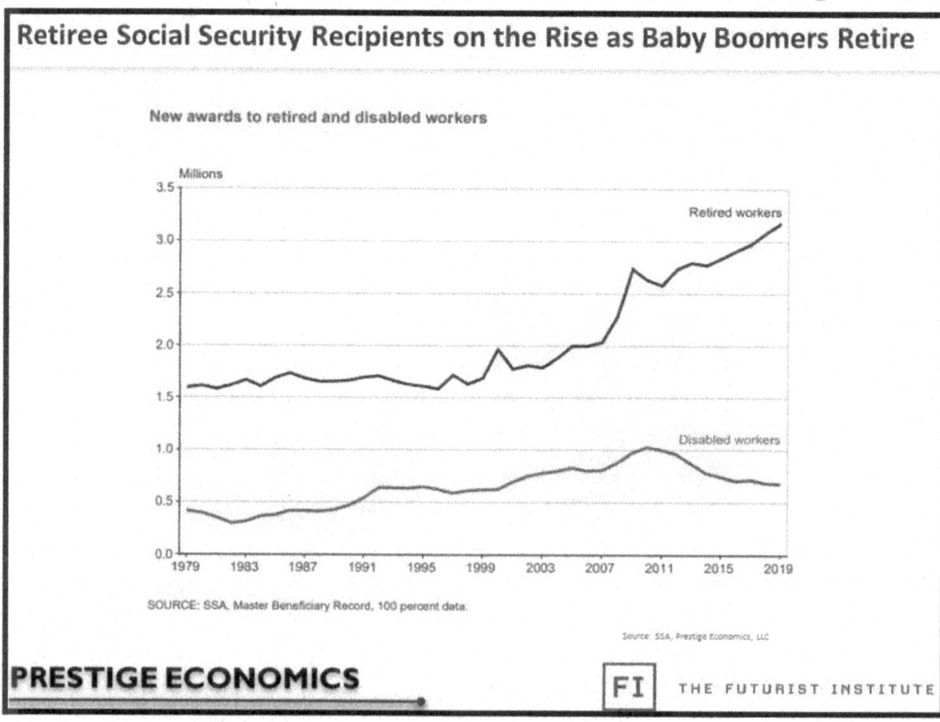

Furthermore, insolvency is expected to be reached in 2035, which is shown in Figure 15-6. The exact verbiage from the Social Security Administration report about insolvency is as follows:

> Social Security is not sustainable over the long term at current benefit and tax rates. In 2010, the program paid more in benefits and expenses than it collected in taxes and other noninterest income, and the 2020 Trustees Report projects this pattern to continue for the next 75 years. The Trustees estimate that the combined OASI and DI trust fund reserves will be depleted by 2035. At that point, payroll taxes and other income will flow into the fund but will be sufficient to pay only about 79% of program costs. As reported in the 2020 Trustees Report, the projected shortfall over the next 75 years is 3.21% of taxable payroll.[10]

Figure 15-6: Social Security Insolvency Ahead[11]

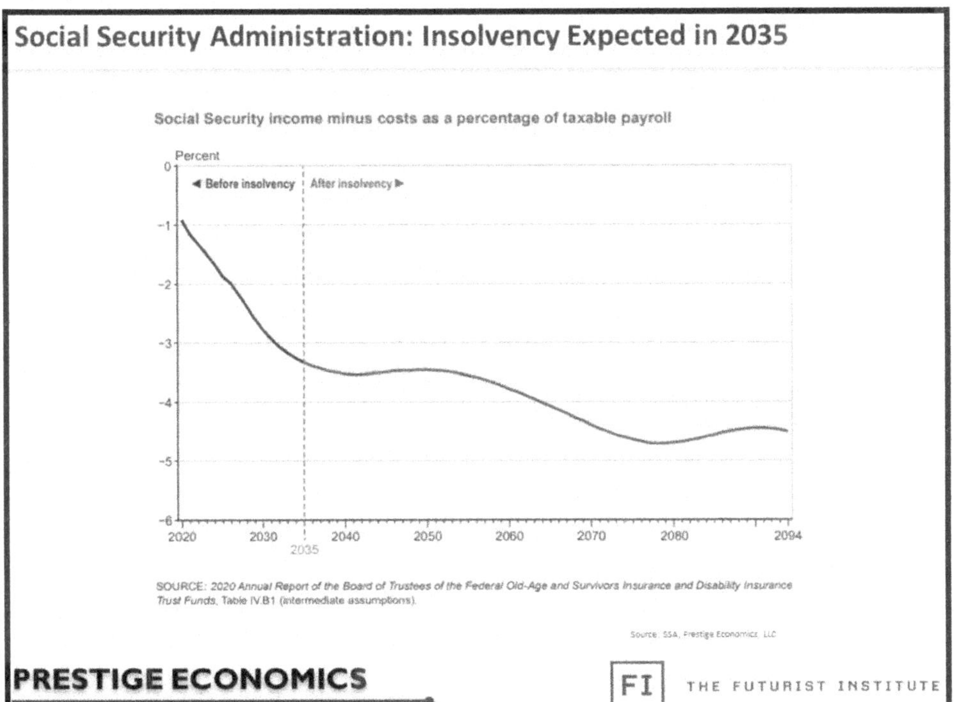

That is a pretty dire warning. But it could actually be worse for two big reasons: even more money is going out *and* less money is coming in than expected.

First, in addition to rising outlays for more retirees who are awarded Social Security, the biggest entitlement risks to the economy and government finances may be Medicare and Medicaid costs. Those costs have been rising sharply and they are likely to be even more elevated in the current environment due to the asymmetric negative impacts of the COVID-19 pandemic on older people, like retirees.

Second, these are just the *expenses* we are talking about. Interest on ever-growing mountains of debt, sky-high unemployment rates with the associated benefits costs, increased Medicare and Medicaid costs, and the cost of Social Security are just one-half of the equation for the government. There's also the income side.

Entitlements financing is likely to be soft for some time to come. After all, with a higher level of unemployment, fewer people will be paying payroll taxes. And since entitlements are funded with revenues from payroll taxes, this could greatly exacerbate the entitlements shortfalls — especially if there is a payroll tax cut to stimulate the economy.

Two Ways

Although some may take comfort in the fact that foreign exchange rates may remain stable because all countries are taking on mountains of debt, the future of global economic growth seems significantly less certain with rapidly rising amounts of government debt.

In fact, the entire situation reminds me of a discussion in Hemingway's novel *The Sun Also Rises*. At one point, a character is asked a question that seems apropos here: "How did you go bankrupt?"

His reply: "Two ways. Gradually, then suddenly."

When I think about the fact that it took the level of U.S. debt 205 years to reach $1 trillion but that the debt has recently risen by about $1 trillion per month in each month of Q2 2020, it seems not unforeseeable that U.S. debt default risk is rising. It also likely means that further significant purchases of government debt by central banks lie ahead.

Beyond the Nation

There is one final piece of the debt puzzle that we need to consider: state debt. It faces greater risks than federal debt. In fact, all government debt aside from national debt faces much greater risks ahead. After all, a national or federal government can print more money or direct its central bank to buy all its debt. For a city, county, or state, however, that's not an option.

Yes, central banks can buy muni debt. We have most certainly seen the Fed go down that road. But these debt issuers are at the mercy of national governments and central banks. And with imminent shortfalls in income, sales, and corporate tax revenues, these entities will be further stressed. Additionally, if unemployment remains high, state government expenses could be higher — and a looming housing crisis could also set in, dampening potential property tax revenues. All of that does not bode well for muni debt.

Demographics

U.S. population growth has slowed sharply, and this demographic shift appears unstoppable. Plus, as birthrates have fallen, life expectancy has also risen. This compounds the funding shortfalls for entitlements. Worse still: No president, senator, or congressman can change U.S. demographics. This is bigger than one person.

And its discussion is unlikely to be anywhere near the 2020 presidential election — and other coming elections as well.

Population growth in the United States has fallen from annual rates of over 1.5 percent per year during the 1950s and early 1960s to just 0.7 percent since 2011.[12] Some of this slowing in population growth is due to a decline in the U.S. fertility rate. In general, fertility rates have been dropping globally, but according to demographer Jonathan Last, the U.S. fertility rate is still relatively high at 1.93.[13]

However, even though the U.S. total fertility rate is relatively high compared to other industrialized nations, it is below the 2.1 percent "golden number" required to maintain a population, according to Last.[14]

This is a huge problem for maintaining entitlements. After all, the entitlement system worked really well in 1940, when there were 159.4 workers per beneficiary (Figure 15-7). But it is more challenging since that number fell to only 2.8 in 2013. Plus, it is likely to fall to 2 workers per beneficiary by 2040.[15]

Everything might be OK — if U.S. population growth were extremely robust. But it is not. Plus, the current administration is pushing hard to reduce illegal immigration to the United States. While this can have some benefits for society and the economy in some ways, it can also reduce the pace of population growth and lower the average U.S. birthrate.

Furthermore, there are growing indications that the COVID-19 recession and pandemic could result in a baby bust, as noted in a July 2020 Bloomberg article by Peter Coy.[16]

Figure 15-7: Ratio of Workers to Social Security Beneficiaries[17]

Year	Covered Workers (in thousands)	Beneficiaries (in thousands)	Ratio
1940	35,390	222	159.4
1945	46,390	1,106	41.9
1950	48,280	2,930	16.5
1955	65,200	7,563	8.6
1960	72,530	14,262	5.1
1965	80,680	20,157	4.0
1970	93,090	25,186	3.7
1975	100,200	31,123	3.2
1980	113,656	35,118	3.2
1985	120,565	36,650	3.3
1990	133,672	39,470	3.4
1995	141,446	43,107	3.3
2000	155,295	45,166	3.4
2005	159,081	48,133	3.3
2010	156,725	53,398	2.9
2013	163,221	57,471	2.8

The risk of debt losing value is significant. It means that those investors who hold fixed income could see their investments become worthless. This is a growing risk for muni debtholders.

Of course, we could also see debt defaults by national and federal governments, but printing money and directing central banks to buy the debt seems more likely. This means that even without explicit defaults, we could see more inflation, which could devalue fixed income payments. Furthermore, given the rising debt levels, it is not inconceivable that we could also see negative interest rates in the future. Such a move could increase the relative value of existing fixed income interest rate products, but it would not provide positive yields on future fixed income investments. It could be quite the opposite if rates go negative.

As for the future of government services and the ability to support the populace through an economic crisis, that potential will become diminished as the federal debt continues to rise. It also means that hopes of universal basic income are very likely folly, because the government will likely soon struggle to pay for entitlements and the interest on its debt, let alone be able to cut endless new checks for people who may or may not be working.

There really seem to be only two ways forward for government expenses. Either interest rates will go negative, and countries (and other debtholders) will perversely earn interest on their debts. Or inflation will become rampant, and the debt will be devalued. In my opinion, since the demand side of the U.S. economy (and other advanced economies) is currently weak, negative rates appear to be more likely than consumer inflation — especially since they already exist in the Eurozone.

CHAPTER 16

CENTRAL BANK BALANCE SHEETS

Once upon a time, there were central banks that had balance sheets that facilitated their day-to-day operations. Sometimes, they raised interest rates to dampen business and fixed investment. Other times, they lowered interest rates to encourage business and fixed investment.

Central banks used deposit rates, interest rates on excess reserves, and other interest rates (like the U.S. federal funds rates) to impact economic growth. But they didn't go into financial markets and buy assets as a means to influence interest rates or keep the economy from coming apart at the seams.

Then, one day, the Great Recession happened. A housing bubble in the United States spilled over into the financial system, causing a crisis. After dropping rates to zero, the only way to revive housing appeared to be by having the central bank buy up mortgages. At the same time, buying government debt also appeared to be a solid way to dampen interest rates to encourage companies facing mortal danger to take risks and make investments. And so it was.

It worked. Boy, did it work. The Fed, European Central Bank, Bank of Japan, and others expanded their balance sheets by essentially pulling money out of the sky to buy assets with maturity dates. The logic was that this short-term buying with money that previously did not exist wouldn't be a problem, because central banks could allow these fixed income products of mortgages, treasuries, and other debt assets to mature and roll off the balance sheet. When that happened, they would turn back into cash — cash that never existed — and vanish altogether.

The Fed expanded its balance sheet from under $900 billion before the Great Recession to over $4.5 trillion by December 2014, as you can see in Figure 16-1.

Figure 16-1: Fed Balance Sheet[1]

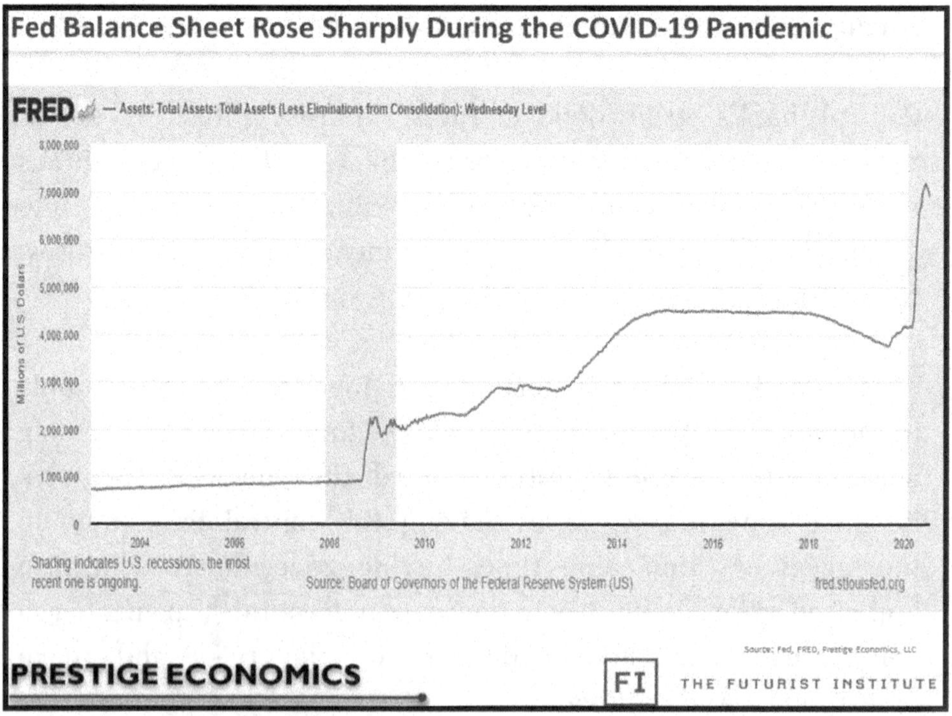

The ECB also expanded its balance sheet by over 1.5 trillion euros through mid-2012, as you can see in Figure 16-2.

Then, the ECB — the progeny of the fiscally conservative BuBa — tried valiantly to shrink its balance sheet between mid-2012 and late 2014 by about 1 trillion euros. It failed miserably.

Yes, the balance sheet shrank, but the Eurozone was almost pushed into a recession. The Fed would also eventually try to shrink its balance sheet (in much smaller percentage terms) during 2018 and 2019. That plan also failed. In fact, the Fed's balance sheet reduction helped cause a business and fixed investment recession in the United States in 2019.

Figure 16-2: ECB Balance Sheet[2]

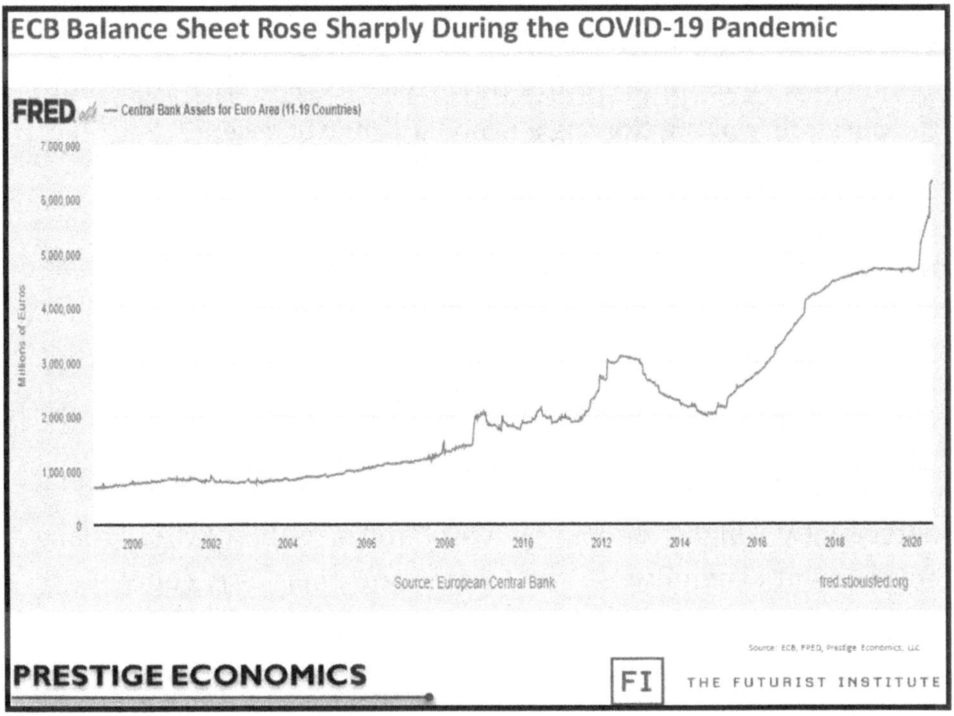

Given the economic aftershocks of these two failed attempts to reduce an expanded central bank balance sheet, it appears as if these balance sheets can only grow. They cannot shrink.

So, when the assets mature, the funds need to be reinvested into financial markets — or economic growth will slow sharply.

In response to the COVID-19 pandemic and recession, central banks have massively expanded their balance sheets. They have been buying a much broader range of assets, and this was completely foreseeable.

In fact, Janet Yellen even noted at the annual Kansas City Fed event in Jackson Hole, Wyoming, in 2016 (when she was the Fed Chair) that "I expect that forward guidance and asset purchases will remain important components of the Fed's policy toolkit." She further added that "future policymakers may wish to explore the possibility of purchasing a broader range of assets."[3]

And here we are. In just a matter of months, the Fed's balance sheet is more than $2.7 trillion greater than it was on 1 January 2020. Along with a massive ballooning of the Fed's balance sheet, U.S. federal funds rates are close to zero as shown in Figure 16-3. But this may not be the bottom for U.S. interest rates.

There are also risks that a housing crisis could be engendered by persistently high unemployment rates. And with rising government expenditures and income shortfalls, it is conceivable that we could see negative interest rates in the United States.

There have been negative rates in the Eurozone since 2014 — not long before the ECB had to backpedal on its balance sheet reduction policy.

Policymakers refer to the use of expanding balance sheets as quantitative easing. Economists refer to it as modern monetary theory — or MMT. But whenever I speak about this topic to clients or in a public speech, I feel like I'm discussing some crazy, fantastical, magical fairy tale. Sometimes I even call it magical monetary theory.

In short, that's not a good sign for sustainability. The question now is, how long can these dynamics reign?

Figure 16-3: U.S. Effective Federal Funds Rate[4]

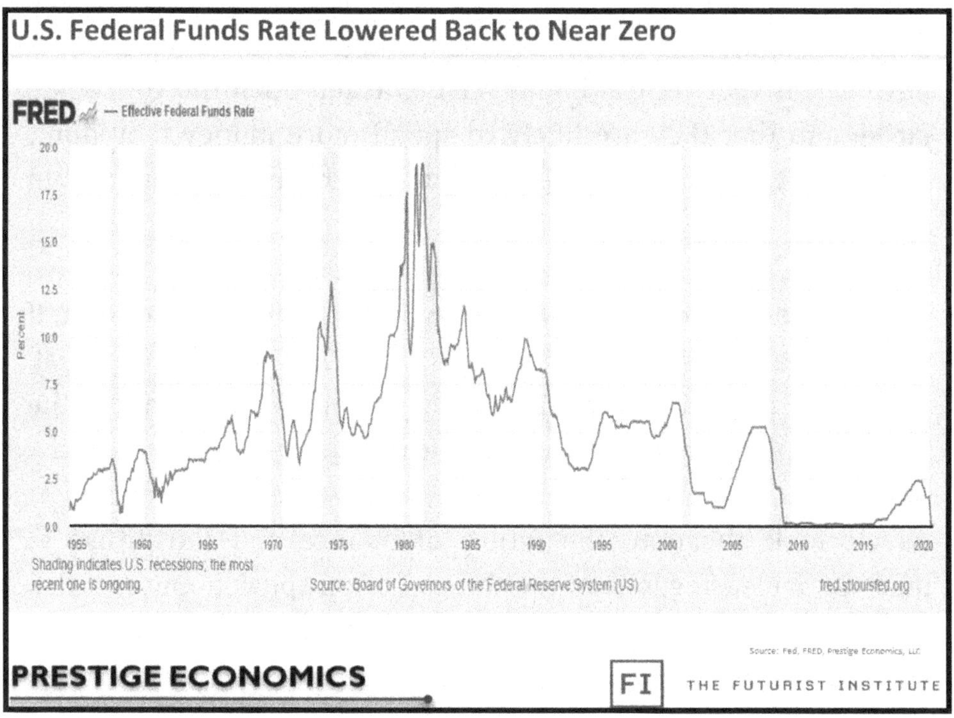

Central Bank Balance Sheets and Cryptocurrencies

The expansion of central bank balance sheets is fundamentally supportive of the economic and financial arguments in favor of Bitcoin and digital currencies that are not backed by central banks. In fact, the first Bitcoin transaction, which is often referred to as the Genesis Block, included the following message:

The Times 03/Jan/2009 Chancellor on brink of second bailout for banks[5]

The Bank of England engaged in multiple bailouts and a 300 percent expansion in the size of its balance sheet between 2007 and 2012.

The impact of these expansions and persistently high levels of central bank balance sheets of the Fed, the BoJ, the ECB and the Bank of England is unclear. What has been clear for some time, however, is that central banks have cracked open the QE cookie jar — and that they are likely to spend more money they don't have, effectively creating the ability to purchase assets out of thin air.

There is no problem, however, from an accounting standpoint, if the assets eventually expire in value and fall off the balance sheet. But that is not going to be the case with the balance sheet of the Bank of Japan, which includes significant equity assets.

As we look ahead to the future of finance and the future of quantitative easing, one of the things I often speak about is a risk that with each cyclical downturn in the future, central banks may continue to expand their balance sheets.

As long as they are all doing this, however, it may not drastically impact foreign exchange rates. After all, if everyone plays the game, it's tougher for there to be an outright winner — or loser.

Plus, they will all want to play the quantitative easing game again if they can, just as they did after the Great Recession and in the wake of the COVID-19 recession.

The Future Quantum State of the U.S. Economy

The dynamics I have just described could eventually result in something I refer to as the future quantum state of the economy. As the U.S. Federal Reserve buys more assets during each downturn with money that it pulled out of nowhere, the central bank's balance sheet will grow and grow. With each cycle, the central bank will become increasingly important as the buyer of last resort so that almost any company or municipality in the entire U.S. economy becomes too big to fail.

This could also become extremely challenging, as the U.S. national debt rises due to unfunded entitlements and interest. One potential worst-case scenario is where the central bank — after decades of cycles — eventually owns almost everything in the economy. And it will have paid for the debt, MBS, Treasuries, equities, and maybe even physical assets on its balance sheet with money it created — with money it didn't have in the first place.

This is effectively how we could have a quantum state of the economy, where the central bank owns everything with nothing. Then we would have a very big problem.

Some analysts have often wondered out loud if there must be a limit to the size of the balance sheet of the Fed or the ECB or the Bank of Japan. But maybe not.

Then there's the question of negative rates. I mean, who's buying bonds that cost them money?

Honestly, I have no answers here.

Time will tell what comes next. But in the world of economics and finance, magical and fantastical off-balance sheet entities are quite inconsistent with durability and sustainability. Still, as traders like to say, markets can remain irrational longer than you can remain solvent.

In terms of options, one thing seems clear. Central banks are coming to the end of the line. Even if rates go negative, they seem unlikely to go significantly negative. This means that the biggest stimulative policies for asset valuations from both quantitative easing and lower interest rates may already be behind us.

Fed Chair Powell was once criticized for using a navigation analogy in the face of uncertain policymaking. But it was apt enough.

Of course, the level of risk to markets, policy, and the economy has significantly ratcheted up since then as a result of the COVID-19 pandemic and recession. And as any good navigator will tell you, when venturing into uncharted territory, it's best to heed the warning of cartographers of yore: Here be dragons.

CHAPTER 17

UNIVERSAL BASIC INCOME

In response to the COVID-19 pandemic, the United States government provided unprecedented levels of stimulus — to businesses and to individuals. This included stimulus payments based on income levels as well as additional, surplus unemployment benefits as part of the CARES Act. In a time when saving hundreds of thousands — or maybe even millions — of American lives was the priority, the country essentially shutdown. And money was spent to keep people afloat.

Some likened it to universal basic income — or UBI. But there is a big difference between planning to make a lot of constant payments to people in an endless stream of free money, and extraordinary emergency measures. It is my opinion that the CARES Act and any additional post-COVID-19 stimulus is not UBI, and that while the stimulus may have helped mitigate some downside risks to the economy, it highlights how UBI may not be effective in some ways, since some people appear to have saved the money, rather than spent it. And for an economy in dire straits, that relies on consumption as 70 percent of GDP, saving is not as critical as spending in a downturn.

What is Universal Basic Income — or UBI?

UBI is the notion that everyone will be paid a flat salary, regardless of whether or not they work. And the biggest problem with universal basic income is that we simply cannot afford it. As you saw in Chapter 15, U.S. entitlement obligations, which could be as high as $200 trillion, make a further expansion of U.S. budgetary obligations for UBI virtually impossible.

According to David Freedman, who wrote an article on the subject for *MIT Technology Review*, an annual payment of $10,000 to every adult American "would be at least twice as expensive as current antipoverty benefits and overhead, adding between one and two trillion dollars to the federal budget."[1]

Furthermore, Freedman argues that "existing safety-net programs could be expanded and tuned to eliminate poverty about as effectively but much less expensively, and they could continue to focus on providing jobs and the incentives to take them."[2] In other words, the inefficient programs in place could be better than UBI. Yikes!

Risks Beyond Cost

Aside from the cost of UBI, which is insurmountable, there are four major problems with UBI:

Inflation would rise.
Taxes would rise.
Long-term economic development could be stifled.
Society could become fractured.

European Attitudes

In Figure 17-1, you can see the results of a survey from a few years ago in which Europeans voiced support for universal basic income. However, despite this support, UBI has so far failed when voters went to the ballot box to vote on the idea. As such, not one single nation has voted to approve this policy.

The entire concept of UBI smacks of full-blown communism, with a redistribution of income. Perhaps this is why Europeans, who have a more colorful political history than Americans, find it to be an appealing option. However, it is more likely that UBI finds support in Europe because the same respondents who support UBI do not actually fully understand it. I believe this is likely also a major issue driving U.S. attitudes toward UBI. The lack of understanding is reflected in Figure 17-2.

Figure 17-1: Europeans Who Would Vote for Basic Income[3]

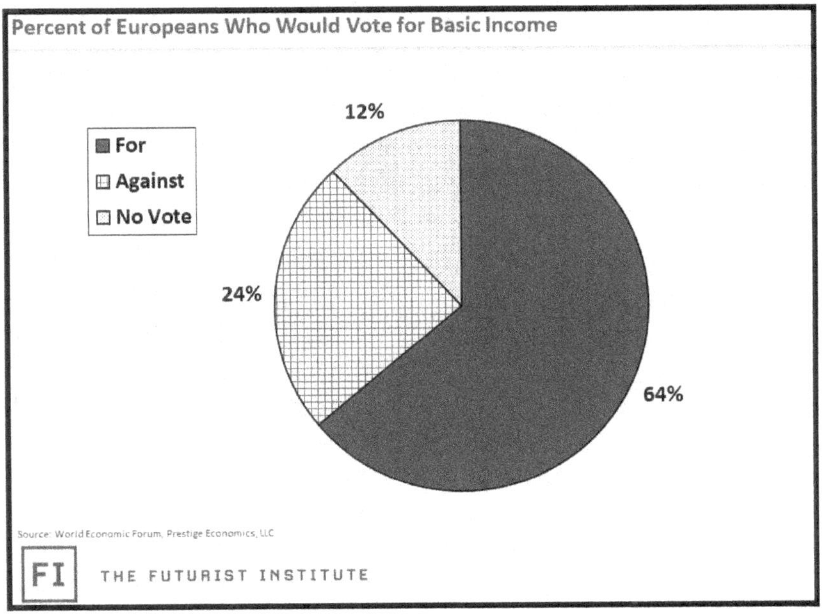

For my European friends, as well as my American ones, let us now consider some costs of UBI that go beyond the budget.

Inflation

Inflation is when prices rise and the dollars you have lose purchasing power. In other words, prices get inflated, and the value of the dollars you own goes down. There has been a secular decline in rates of year-over-year inflation in the United States since it peaked in June 1979, as you can see in Figure 17-3.

Now, imagine for a second, what would happen if everyone got UBI? This is basically free money, and everyone gets it. What would happen to the price of a cup of coffee, a car, clothes, or food if every single adult received a handout from the government for doing nothing?

Figure 17-2: Europeans Familiar With Basic Income[4]

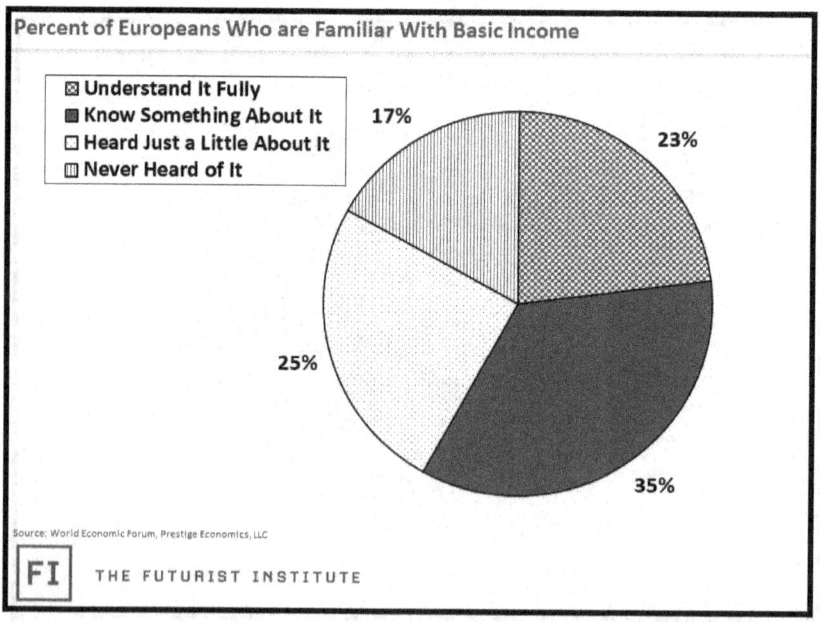

How much is a Honda when everyone is handed half a Honda in free income for doing nothing every year?

The logical outcome seems pretty straightforward: Prices would rise. Higher rates of inflation are good for asset holders and debt holders, but they are particularly bad for people on fixed income.

For now, in the wake of the COVID-19 pandemic and recession, inflation rates are exceptionally low. This is a normal result of very high unemployment and recession. When people don't have jobs, they don't spend money because they don't have money. Even with the CARES Act stimulus, people were clearly afraid to spend money, and this kept inflation under pressure as well.

Figure 17-3: U.S. Consumer Price Inflation Rate[5]

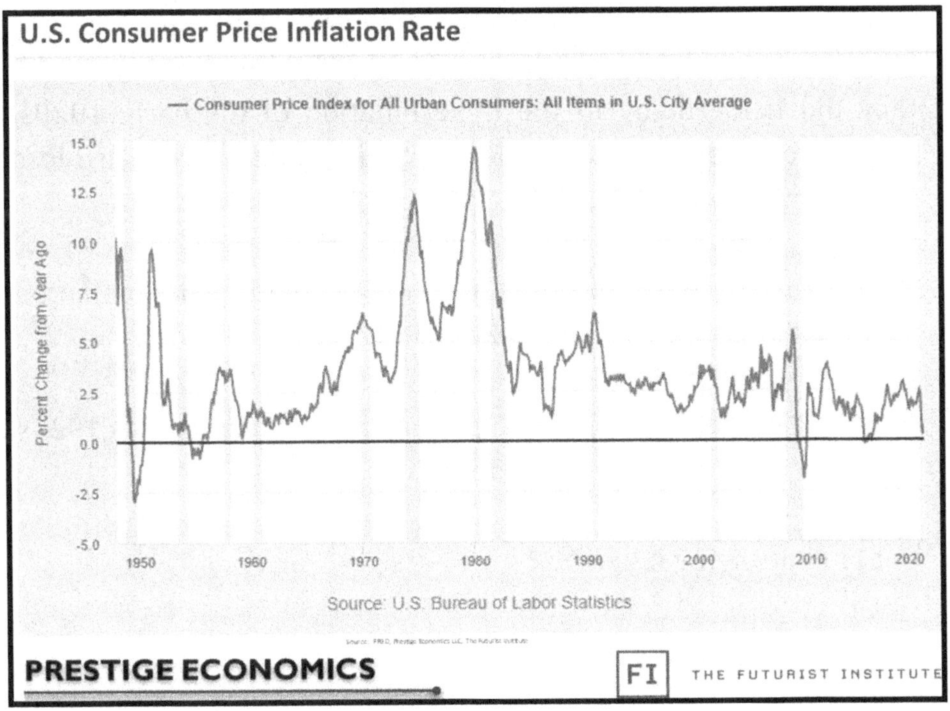

Fixed income investments include corporate bonds and Treasuries, as well as Social Security and defined benefits pensions. Given the risk of inflation from UBI, the minute people get UBI income and begin spending it, prices would rise, and those fixed income payments would be devalued.

As prices rise, the need to increase UBI would also rise to offset the loss of value from inflation. This would, in turn, send prices even higher, justifying the need to further increase UBI. And so forth and so on. So how much is enough?

The truth is that once we go down the path of UBI, no amount may be enough. The printing presses of the future will need to digitally issue new money for UBI at an ever-quickening pace.

Low, stable inflation is conducive to growth, and high levels of inflation can make an economy unstable. If prices rise rapidly, as they did in Germany in the hyperinflation of the early 1920s, people could end up wallpapering their homes with worthless paper currency.

To use a more recent example, paper bills could be denominated in the trillions, like they are in Zimbabwe.

Now, I'm not saying UBI would put us on the same path as 1920s Germany or modern-day Zimbabwe.

But I'm not saying it won't.

Taxes Would Rise

Since we cannot afford to pay for UBI with the current U.S. government budget and we cannot afford to drive up our national debt by another $1 to $2 trillion (in today's value) annually, we would need to find the money for UBI somewhere else. We could just print it, but that means running up the debt; we can't surreptitiously run dollar printing presses, sneaking bags of UBI into everyone's home while they sleep like some kind of income Santa. But that is likely the plan most people are going with. Better stock up on milk and cookies now!

But in all seriousness, there is only one way to get the money that would be needed for UBI: taxes. It could be higher payroll taxes, higher corporate taxes, higher property taxes, or the creation of some new taxes, like a robotic labor payroll tax. But one thing is certain: Taxes would rise.

No matter what your view on UBI, we can probably all agree on one thing: Corporations (and individuals) respond to tax incentives. And higher taxes that are implemented to purely redistribute wealth without any labor or activity requirement on the part of the recipient would reduce incentives for technological development, investment, and economic activity.

Payroll Taxes on Robots

The debate about a payroll tax on robots has heated up, and a number of business leaders, including Bill Gates, have voiced support for such a policy. But defining which jobs are affected will be a challenge. Would it be for robots *and* computers? For hardware and software? For smartphones and Microsoft Excel?

The debate over a robot payroll tax is unlikely to go away, but its implementation, and the allocation of associated tax revenues, could be complicated. But a robot payroll tax is likely to be something that policymakers look at more closely over time, especially if a high number of jobs are automated out of existence.

Of course, the money from a robot payroll tax *could* be earmarked to fulfill the unfunded entitlement obligations of Medicare, Medicaid, and Social Security. After all, these are already funded by payroll taxes. But even with a robot payroll tax, policymakers may neglect to fund entitlement obligations, because if robot payroll taxes go to fund entitlements, there may not be much wiggle room to implement UBI.

Although I am very skeptical of the concepts of a robot payroll tax and universal basic income, one thing in the world of politics always rings true: When you rob Peter to pay Paul, you can always count on Paul's vote. In this case, Peter would be a robot without a vote. And Paul would get free money.

Corporate Taxes

As part of the U.S. tax reform of 2017, U.S. corporate tax rates were lowered. It was lauded as stimulative for corporate profits, for investments, and the economy. But a future move to significantly raise corporate tax rates to finance the UBI free handout for every American would likely meet with sharp resistance — and corporate relocations. The U.S. economy would likely experience a mass exodus of corporations that would seek to avoid UBI taxation. They would just leave.

Of course, we could single out technology corporations, but technology companies have a 5x multiplier on job creation.[6]

Want to see the UBI needs balloon quickly? Scare away companies at which each job created is capable of supporting the creation of five additional jobs.

Taxes on Income Assets

Another way to finance UBI would be to tax people who work. Yes, everyone gets free UBI money. But the people who also get paid to work will pay for everyone else to get the UBI money — even if none of the other recipients work, want to work, or ever plan to work.

They will even pay UBI for the recipients who just want to play some future virtual reality holodeck version of Xbox their entire lives. This leads us to our next topic and the negative risks to long-term economic development from implementing such a UBI system.

Death and Taxes — or at Least Taxes

Before closing out this section, I want to note that there are currently two guarantees in life: death and taxes. Singularitarians and Transhumanists, like Zoltan Istvan, would tell you that death is not guaranteed in the future. In the future you may be able to live forever. However, taxes are still going to be guaranteed.

And with the implementation of UBI, *higher* taxes would also be guaranteed.

Negative Long-Run Economic Impacts

During the industrial revolution — at the onset of the age of iron and steel — factories decimated the occupations of smiths, weavers, and many others.

Of course, there were also very unpleasant times during the Industrial Revolution. There were widespread abuses of the labor force, including child labor, horrific working conditions, and a lack of worker protection.

This led to the creation of unions and resulted in labor reforms. Things like weekends, holidays, and paid vacations came from the development of unions, and a push toward more humane working environments proved to be successful as well.

These problems may have been imperfectly fixed, but society improved, and the economy progressed.

At the same time that village life was fully eroding, the emergence and creation of new professions also became critical. And broader access to university-level education helped train more doctors, journalists, lawyers, and other professionals. And there were great improvements across a number of professions and industries, which had very positive impacts on society.

But what would have happened if people had just stayed in their villages and they had just been given a handout?

Medieval Universal Basic Income

Imagine if 1800s European monarchs had decided to just hand out money to smiths, millers, and weavers to never work again. What would have happened to European growth? What if these tradesmen had managed to wrangle UBI out of the U.S. government in the late 1800s? What would have happened to the U.S. economy?

I suspect that such policies would have caused economies to suffer from significant underperformance, stifled economic development, and slow growth.

With such negative ramifications, why are people talking about UBI now?

UBI does not help individuals bridge skills gaps. It just avoids the problem by throwing money at it. But in doing so, it short circuits the adaptive nature of capitalist economies, and it reduces the longer-term potential for economic growth. This is something we need to think about in relation to UBI. If everyone just gets a handout, the economy will stop adapting — it will stop growing.

More importantly, there is an individual cost to UBI as a solution to permanent job loss. If individuals in the late 1800s had been given money because their jobs ceased to exist — because society had changed — what would have happened to those individual smiths, millers, tanners, and weavers if they had done nothing? Would they have also felt that they were nothing? What would have happened to society at that point? And what will happen to ours if people do nothing and receive UBI now?

German Shepherds

While a number of jobs over time are going to change and become obsolete, I fundamentally believe that humans will need things to do and that entire lives of unearned leisure are not exactly lives of pure contentment. Yes, a lot of years of leisure is nice. But have you ever wondered why billionaires continue to work? It's because they are German shepherds.

Most people I know — my family, close friends, and even acquaintances — remind me of German shepherds. They like to have things to do. They like to be busy and occupied. Anyone who has ever owned a German shepherd, watched a German shepherd, or volunteered in an animal shelter knows that if these dogs don't have enough to do, they'll destroy the furniture in their own house out of sheer boredom. It is my fundamental belief that people without enough to do will also rip up their own lives just to avoid being bored.

This is also a key lesson of Greek mythology. Greek gods and goddesses got into wars and conflicts because they were bored. With nothing to do, they wreaked havoc on the world for no reason other than sheer boredom. We should be concerned.

It's one thing when retirees receive entitlements, because they are generally less physically active. But it's another thing entirely when young adults are unoccupied; they need things to do. This could be a challenge in a future with more robots and automation. Without a way to keep people mentally and physically active, there are risks to society. It is a threat people don't think about — and they certainly don't talk about it.

Idle hands are the work of the devil. For this reason, it is going to be a very big problem if people don't have something to do. A world without work — a world of UBI — presents existential risks to society. And this will impact finance as well.

As Kaplan pointed out in his book on robots and the future of work, *Humans Need Not Apply*, "Money is not the only reason to work. People like to feel that they are useful members of society. They enjoy making a contribution to the welfare of others in addition to providing for themselves and their families. Most people feel great satisfaction in helping others, increasing their sense of self-worth, and giving their lives purpose and meaning."[7]

Figure 17-4: Busy People are Happy People[8]

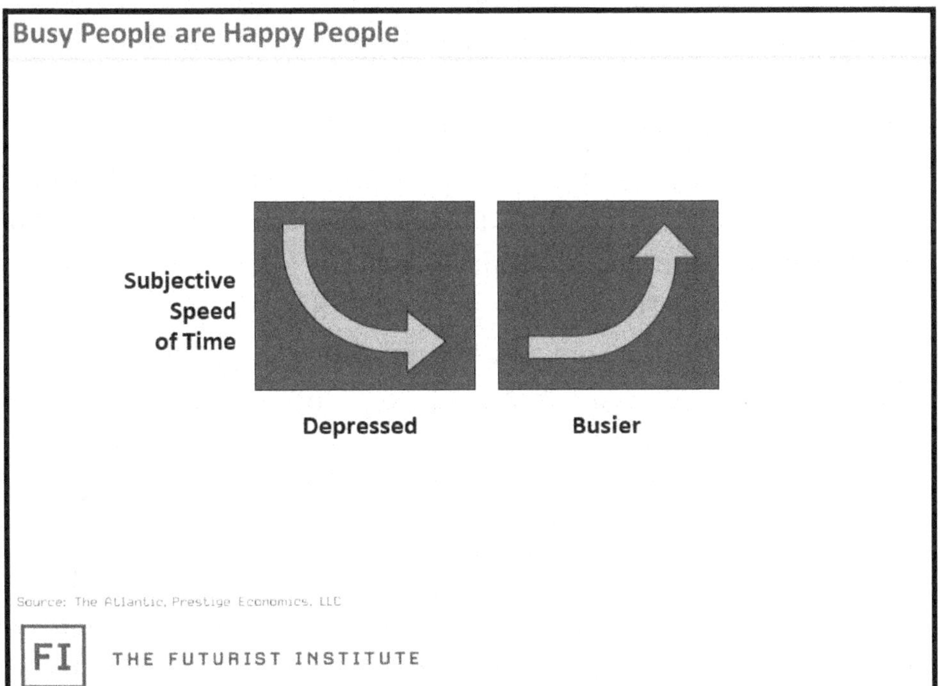

I have long said that busy people are happy people, which was a concept reinforced by an article in *The Atlantic* from February 2017, which included Figure 17-4.[9] Another *The Atlantic* writer noted that "The paradox of work is that many people hate their jobs, but they are considerably more miserable doing nothing."[10]

The Grandfather of Universal Basic Income

When the Berlin Wall fell in 1989 and the Soviet Union subsequently collapsed in 1991, the West declared that capitalism had defeated communism. But the view of history changes with time. After all, it is now accepted by most historians of European history that World War I and World War II were one war with a lengthy armistice between two periods of actual armed conflict. I must then wonder if we have actually seen the end of communism or if we are merely lodged in a period of armistice.

After all, if universal basic income makes it across the finish line of history, we may come to view the "end" of the Cold War as just Round 1 of a struggle that capitalism could still lose. I have read the works of communist leaders such as Marx, Engels, Lenin, Luxemburg, and Trotsky. Yet some of their writings are less aggressive than the language used by some Silicon Valley executives when they speak about a post-capitalist Robotopia.

Make no mistake: The final judgement on the failure of communism may not yet have been written. And while Otto von Bismarck is considered the grandfather of U.S. Social Security by the U.S. Social Security Administration, I think we need to recognize that Karl Marx is the grandfather of universal basic income.

Figure 17-5: Grandfather of Universal Basic Income, Karl Marx[11]

The costs of universal basic income would be very high. UBI could lead to rampant inflation, an exodus of businesses, higher taxes, long-term economic stagnation, and a fracturing of individual lives and society. Universal basic income is not a viable choice. We must adapt to change.

Ascending Politics of Universal Basic Income

I first wrote about UBI in *Jobs for Robots* (2017). I subsequently had a number of interactions with proponents of UBI.

Many of these have been unpleasant.

Free money is an alluring offer, and I expected back in early 2017 that the number of people who think UBI is a great idea would rise sharply in the years to come. I even noted that UBI is likely to be one of the hottest political issues of the coming two decades. Indeed, this expectation has already proven to be correct.

In 2019, there was one presidential candidate touting the notion of UBI as a main part of his presidential campaign. But in the wake of the COVID-19 pandemic and the CARES Act, some people have become accustomed to free money. This means that we are likely to see the idea of UBI gain traction in the future among multiple candidates running for president in the United States.

Even if the U.S. economy cannot afford it, free money for everyone could captivate a large swath of the American population. Plus, UBI proponents might even be able to find support for a rallying cry, *"Non-workers of the world unite!"*

We must resist the siren song of free money because the false promise of UBI could sink the entire economy. Unfortunately, however, UBI is likely to be a topic that will come to the fore in the United States and globally in the coming decade and beyond, not least of all because Pandora's Box was opened during the COVID-19 shutdown as a way to preserve both the public health and the economy at the same time. As of August 2020, the economy is still in tatters, and the CARES Act experience is now poised to taint U.S. political discourse about UBI and the distribution of government finances for decades to come.

CHAPTER 18

GLOBAL UPSIDE OF FINTECH

One of the biggest potential positive economic impacts at the population level for FinTech isn't the marginal changes most banked individuals in developed economies could see in terms of lower costs and ease of use. The big promise of FinTech on a global scale is democratized access.

And the biggest value adds are likely to be — and remain — in emerging markets, where access to financial institutions, banks, and investments has historically been much more limited.

If you live in the United States or another OECD country, it may be difficult to imagine that there are a massive number of unbanked individuals in emerging markets — let alone that there are some at home in the United States as well. But it's true.

Globally, 1.7 billion adults are unbanked. Furthermore, according to the World Bank, about half of these people live in just seven countries: Bangladesh, China, India, Indonesia, Mexico, Nigeria, and Pakistan. You can see the full map in Figure 18-1.[1]

Even in the United States, there are 8.4 million unbanked households. This means that about 6.5 percent of households are completely unbanked — and have no bank accounts of any kind — according to the Federal Deposit Insurance Corporation.[2]

Plus, there are an additional 24.2 million underbanked U.S. households. According to the FDIC, this means that 18.7 percent of all U.S. households have "a checking or savings account but also obtained financial products and services outside of the banking system."[3]

This means that even in the United States, 33 million households — 25.2 percent of households — are unbanked or underbanked.

Figure 18-1: Number of Unbanked Adults Globally[4]

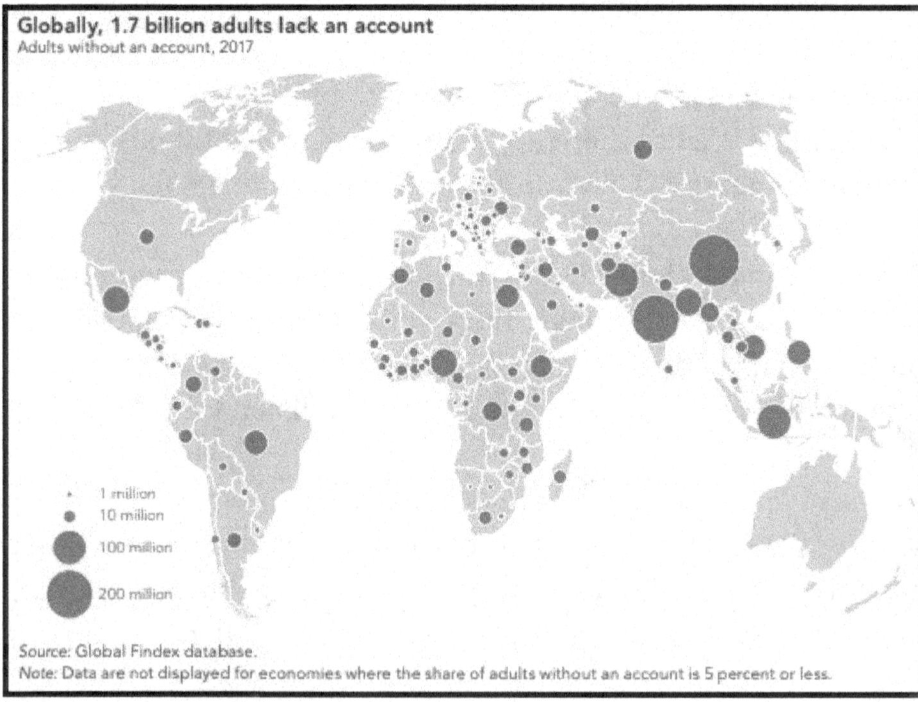

One of the main means to foster greater global access to finance is tied to tapping into the number of unbanked adults that have phones. According to the World Bank, two-thirds of unbanked adults have phones. And this offers promise for increasing the number of banked individuals by using FinTech solutions that can reach those unbanked individuals through their phones.

In a June 2019 report, the IMF noted that FinTech is "having global impact on the provision of financial services" and that "mobile payments have been a key early developer with broad implications for inclusion." Among the big successes, the report explicitly underscored that Africa has seen "rapid growth in mobile money as a driver for greater financial inclusion."[5]

Figure 18-2: Two-Thirds of Unbanked Adults Have Phones[6]

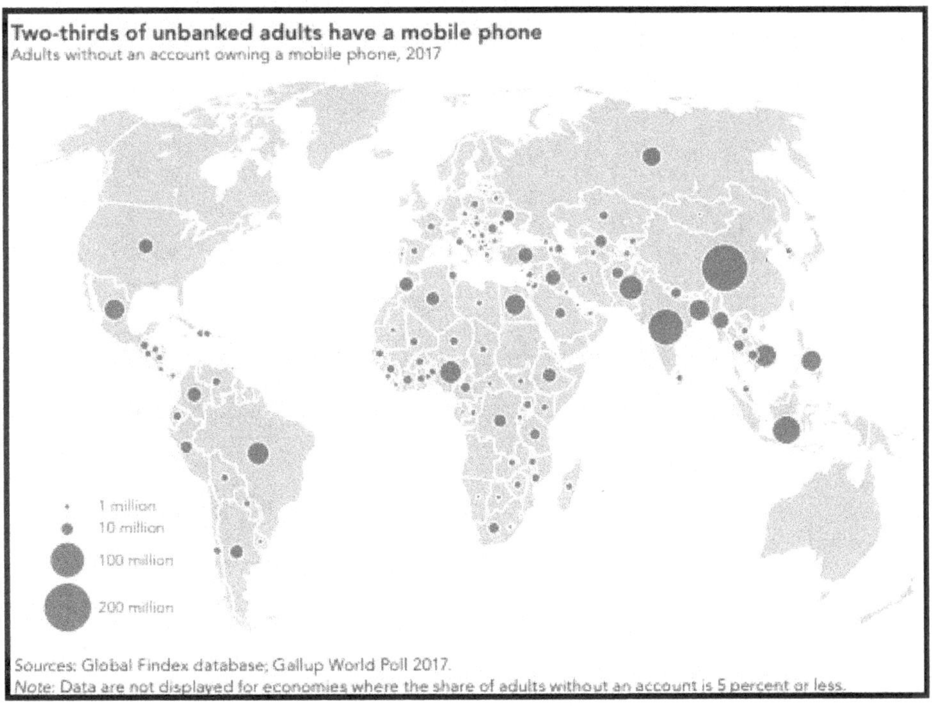

Similarly, the massive spread and adoption of mobile payments in Africa is also something that was highlighted in a 2017 World Bank report. There is a map of adoption showing the swift rise in the percent of adults in Sub-Saharan Africa that made mobile money accounts between 2014 and 2017 in Figure 18-3.

As we look at the future of FinTech, all eyes are on those unbanked and underbanked individuals in emerging markets — and at home. The future of finance will include bringing many of those individuals into the fold of banking, investments, and payments. And it is likely to be a critical priority for FinTech and traditional financial services companies developing or acquiring FinTech solutions to tap into that 1.7 billion person market.

Figure 18-3: Mobile Payments Spread in Africa[7]

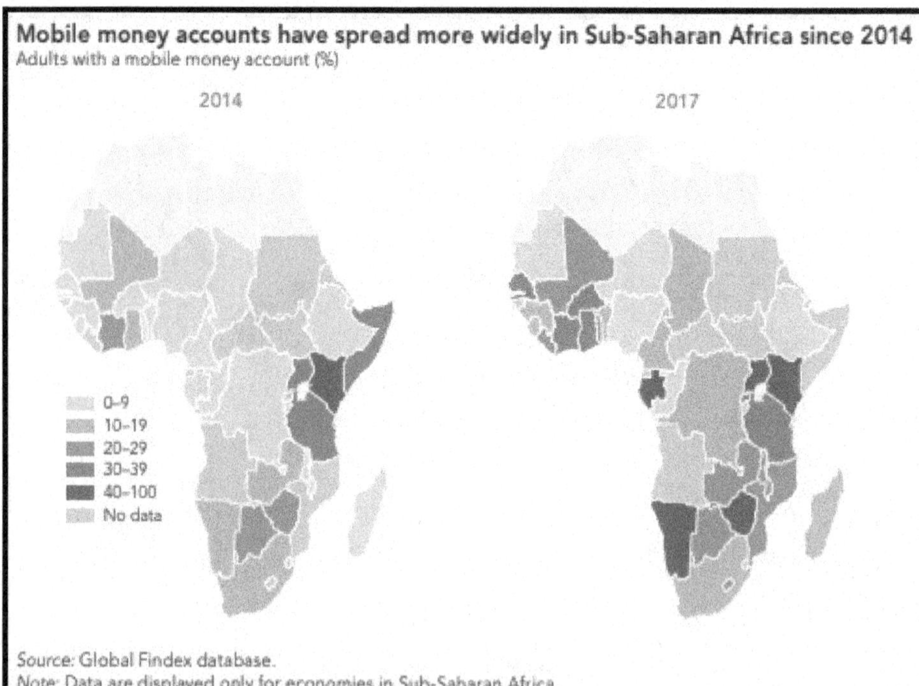

CHAPTER 19

ESG AND SUSTAINABILITY

One of the big trends for the future of finance is a push to incorporate environmental, social, and governance (ESG) goals along with sustainability. This is a trend that has been underway for some years and in the wake of the COVID-19 pandemic and shutdown, many companies have drastically reduced their carbon footprints. People are traveling less and commuting less, and there may be incentives for companies to show ESG progress that could keep many people working from home — and keep travel depressed for many years after the greatest COVID-19 fears have faded.

In 2018, some of the top areas where there were activist investors pushing for goals and initiatives included climate change (19%), sustainability (13%), other environmental (7%), and political activity (19%).[1] You can see the breakdown in Figure 19-1. If we consider sustainability a type of environmental initiative along with climate change and other environmental resolutions, we see that 39% — a plurality — of all activist investor resolutions filed in 2018 were environment related.

I want to be careful here on one point. I am not putting a value judgement on these resolutions. I merely wish to show that they were a plurality of activist investor resolutions in 2018 — and that they are likely to become increasingly important in finance.

Activist investors are usually large investors that use their shareholder power to push companies to make fundamental changes in the way they operate. Their activities have been on the rise. In fact, the number of companies subject to activist demands globally rose by almost 54 percent between 2013 and 2018. This can be seen in Figure 19-2. Domestically, the situation is very similar, and the number of U.S. companies subject to activist demands in 2018 was up by over 50 percent since 2013. This can be seen in Figure 19-3.

Figure 19-1: Type of Activist Resolutions Filed in 2018[2]

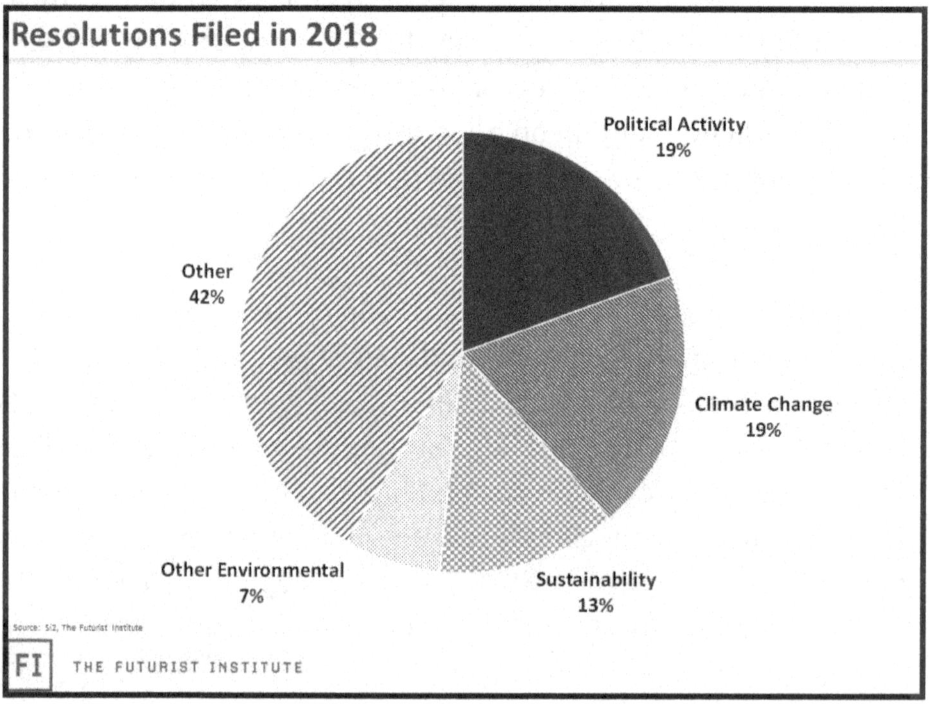

Figure 19-2: Global Companies Subject to Activist Demands[3]

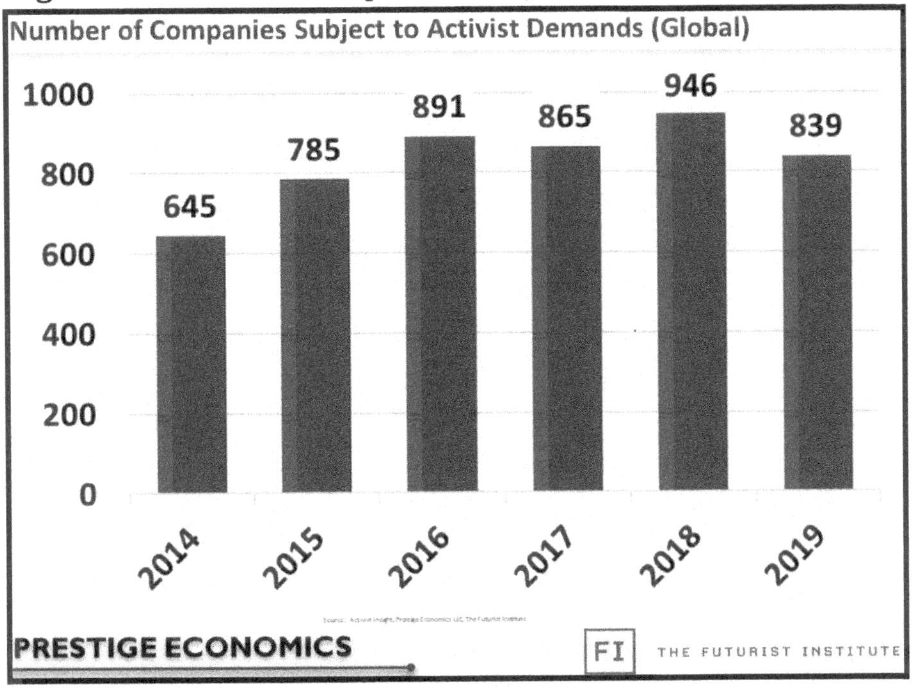

Figure 19-3: U.S. Companies Subject to Activist Demands[4]

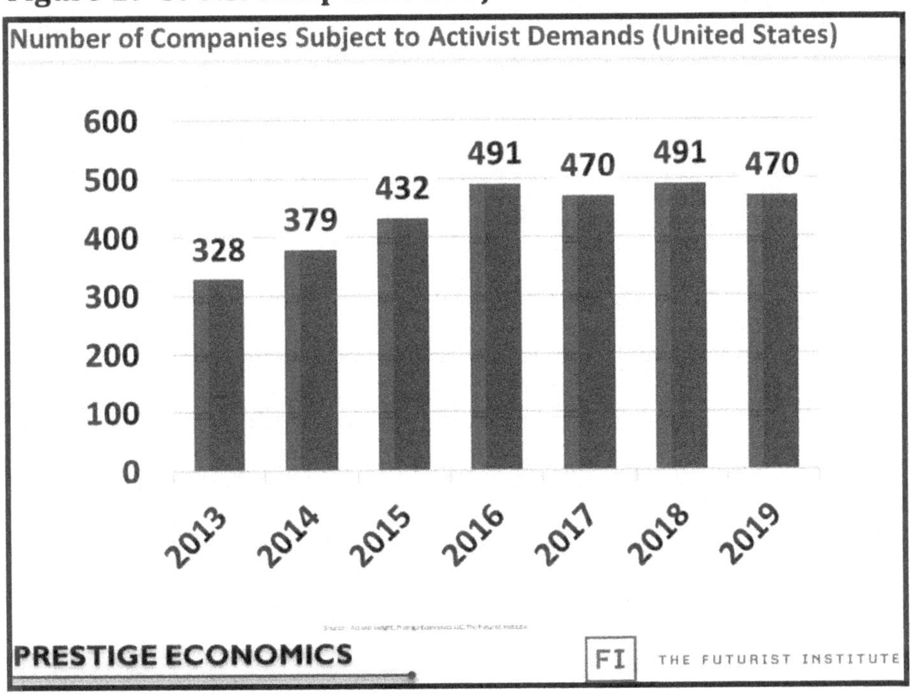

Although activist investor demands fell in the United States and globally in 2019, a long-term rising trend seems likely to continue. Looking at the future of finance, I expect that this dynamic of rising activist demands — and the number of companies impacted — is likely to continue rising on trend.

Companies often benefit from things they don't pay for but that have costs. These costs that are not captured but are passed on to society at large are called externalities. These include any potentially negative environmental impact a business's operations have. But they can also involve leveraging certain labor, societal, or political inefficiencies to capture an arbitrage opportunity to reap outsized financial benefits. The data shows there is a push to make companies price-in these externalities.

But here's the deal: Fully pricing in externalities to company operations is likely to erode profitability for some companies. And that may be just the beginning. Ratings agencies have already started warning companies that their sustainability goals (or lack thereof) could impact their bond prices and their weighted average cost of capital — their WACC.[5] This could in turn impact their profitability, overall valuation, credit rating, and equity prices.

In the future, companies will increasingly need to demonstrate achievable sustainability and other ESG goals. If they don't, they will be at the mercy of activist investors, and their profitability and share prices may suffer. This is why some key changes in corporate expenditures, use of office space and utilities, and reduced commuting could become permanent after COVID-19.

CHAPTER 20

THE IMPORTANCE OF TRADE

The great power competition between the United States and China presents risks to finance, the global economy, and trade. All of these dynamics could significantly impact financial markets as well as global supply chains long after the COVID-19 recession.

We had already started to see these conflict dynamics before the pandemic. Now, there are risks that we are well on our way to embarking on the Second Cold War. Key trade risks between the U.S. and China contributed to a slowing of global growth in 2018 and 2019. This followed strong global growth in 2017, which was supported by strong global trade. But there is more at play between the United States and China than just tariffs. There is a struggle for global economic, political, and military hegemony.

This is why, in part, the U.S.-China trade conflict remains largely unresolved as of August 2020. Furthermore, there are rising risks that the conflict could continue and proliferate further. As that occurs, the downside risks to overall global economic growth will increase. I have previously noted that this may require bifurcated supply chains to serve U.S. and China end markets in the future.

The COVID-19 pandemic has opened the aperture in many ways, revealing open secrets and overlooked risks — for society, the global economy, and national security. For supply chains, COVID-19 has revealed the risks of overly lean U.S. supply chains as well as the potential downside of being dependent on a global supply chain for critical goods like medical supplies, medical devices, basic necessities, and personal protective equipment (PPE), including gloves and masks.

One of the most critical questions now is, how will international relations between China and the United States change — and how could it create ripple effects in global supply chains, the global economy, and great power competition? I recently tried to answer this question by presenting scenarios for the future of supply chain after COVID-19 in an unclassified Pentagon report.

You can download the full unclassified Pentagon report here:
http://www.futuristinstitute.org/pentagon-report/

As we consider the importance of trade for the future of finance, we need to recognize that global economic growth is highly sensitive to global trade. And there are broader global macroeconomic risks in a high-risk trade environment.

After all, as goes the global economy, so goes finance and financial markets. Equity markets also took big hits when the U.S.-China trade war kicked off in early 2018. Plus, the global economy slowed sharply even before the COVID-19 pandemic. Furthermore, If the conflict between these two great powers becomes tenser, as seems likely, growth and financial markets could come under pressure again in the future.

CONCLUSION

THE FUTURE OF FINANCE AFTER COVID

My goal in writing this book was to share visions for the future of finance after the COVID-19 pandemic, shutdown, and recession. Following my discussions of how markets, technology, risks, government and central bank policies, and long-term global dynamics are likely to play out in the decade ahead and beyond, I hope that you now have an understanding of some of the top-line risks and opportunities ahead.

The disruptive nature of the trends that were already underway before the COVID-19 pandemic have been accelerated by the pandemic. Changes in financial services, FinTech, and financial markets will play out in impactful ways for individuals, companies, and entire industries. Perhaps the most disruptive impact will be in the structure of the future financial company.

In short, there will be a lot more people focused on technology, and there will be far fewer people doing what we think of as traditional financial services jobs. This will impact banking, insurance, financial planning, and the rest. You can see one forecast of the impact on financial services jobs in Figure 21-1.

In a number of my books, I have often noted that the companies that will survive and thrive in the current and future era of disruptive innovations will be technology companies at their core. This is likely to be the fate of finance and financial services firms as well.

Historically speaking, education has been the great divider for jobs. In Figure 21-2, you can see statistics on unemployment and earnings from 2019 from the U.S. Bureau of Labor Statistics. Education is positively correlated with income, and education is also inversely correlated with unemployment. In other words, generally speaking, the more education you have, the more money you make and the lower the chance you are unemployed.

Figure 21-1: Forecasted Financial Institution Staff Reductions[1]

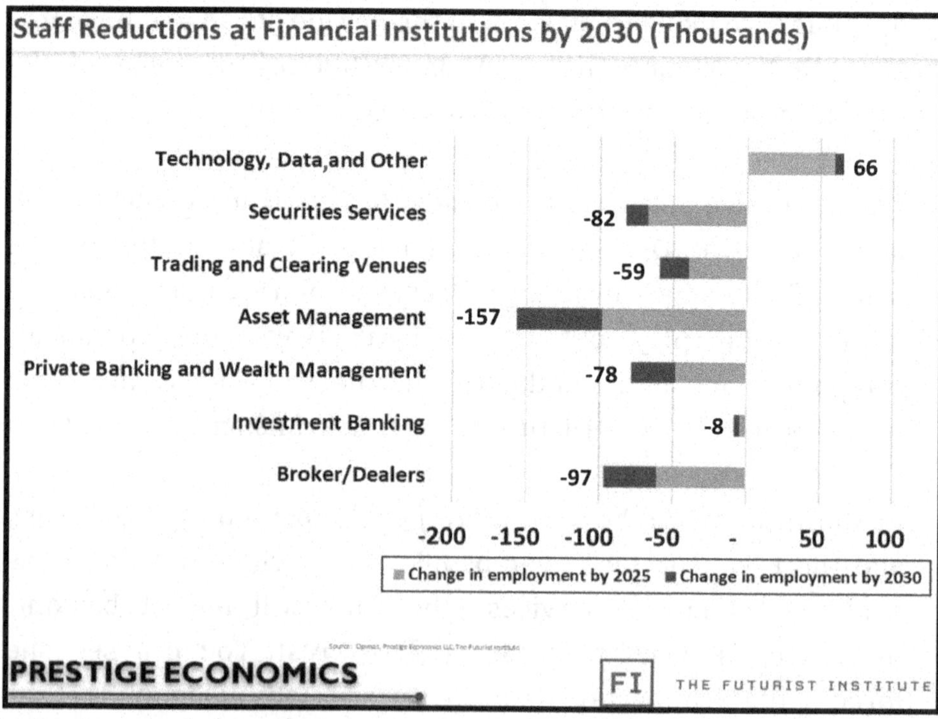

Looking ahead to the future of finance, we still expect that education will remain a critical deciding factor that impacts employability and wages — even if disruption and a massive job shake-up comes to the financial world after the COVID-19 pandemic and recession. But those future job opportunities may be in different areas. People will need to rely on their ability to learn new, technology-focused skills to advance in their careers.

Additionally, it is important to note that some parts of high finance will very much remain a closed network in which education and other accoutrements of professional achievement are conditio sine qua non to be part of the game. In other words, for some parts of finance, FinTech will not be a substitute.

Figure 21-2: Education, Earnings, and Unemployment[2]

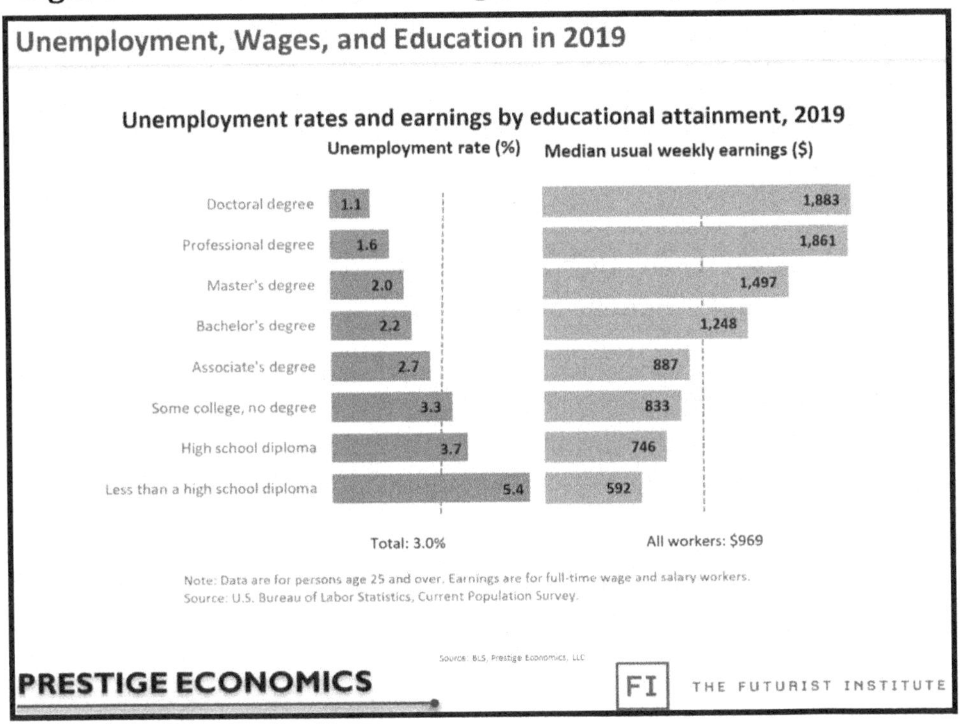

Credit and Business Risks

Even though COVID-19 appears to be a once in a century event, there are likely to be significant long-term impacts for business credit, finance, and cash management.

The reason?

Despite all of the recent Fed bond buying and debt purchases, there are significant risks that companies may face tougher access to credit in the future after the COVID-19 pandemic, shutdown, and recession. In the same way that individuals were more closely scrutinized after the housing crisis and the Great Recession of 2007 to 2009, businesses could experience a tightening of credit following the COVID-19 recession that lasts for years. In the future, banks may be less likely to extend business credit unless companies can demonstrate that they have a significant emergency cash reserve on hand in the event that another pandemic or catastrophic event necessitates a shutdown of the entire economy.

This kind of credit tightening could slow business growth, investment, and economic activity in the recovery years ahead.

Further Learning

If you've enjoyed this book and you want to learn more about planning strategically for an uncertain future, the Certified Futurist and Long-Term Analyst™ — FLTA™ — training program at The Futurist Institute helps leaders incorporate trend and technology risks and opportunities into long-term strategic planning.

The FLTA™ has six distinct professional tracks, including consulting, national security, financial planning, accounting, legal, and standard professional. Plus, The Futurist Institute is accredited as a continuing education provider by the Certified Financial Planner Board of Standards®. Details about the FLTA™ and The Futurist Institute are online at www.futuristinstitute.org.

Your Next Steps

The future of finance will bring opportunities, risks, and challenges. But now that you have been informed of some of the biggest trends that will drive financial services, FinTech, and financial markets in the decade ahead, you can take action.

You are the master of your own destiny, and it's up to you to stay one step ahead of the crowd. Because if you do, there could be big rewards in store. After all, in finance, money is made at the margin. And now you've got more than a little edge to profit in *The Future of Finance After COVID*!

~ Jason Schenker
August 2020

ENDNOTES

Chapter 3

1. Rooney, Kate. (17 June 2020). "Fintech app Robinhood is driving a retail trading renaissance during the stock market's wild ride." CNBC. Retrieved on 15 August 2020 from https://www.cnbc.com/2020/06/17/robinhood-drives-retail-trading-renaissance-during-markets-wild-ride.html.

Chapter 4

1. "Listed Domestic Companies, Total." *Data*, World Bank, data.worldbank.org/indicator/CM.MKT.LDOM.NO?locations=US.
2. Ritter, Jay R. "IPO Data." *Warrington College of Business*, University of Florida. Retrieved on 15 August 2020 from site.warrington.ufl.edu/ritter/ipo-data/.
3. Ibid.
4. Ibid.
5. Ibid.
6. Ibid.

Chapter 7

1. "Widespread Fraud Found in Cryptocurrency Offerings." (April 10, 2018). Texas State Securities Board. Retrieved on 24 August 2018 from https://www.ssb.texas.gov/sites/default/files/CRYPTO%20report%20April%2010%202018.pdf.
2. "Bitcoin (USD) Price." Coindesk. Retrieved on 12 August 2020 from https://www.coindesk.com/price/.
3. "What is Bitcoin? Google Trends Search" Google Trends. Retrieved on 12 August 2020 from https://trends.google.com/trends/explore?q=What%20is%20Bitcoin%3F&geo=US.
4. Katz, L. (1 August 2018). "Long Blockchain Gets Hit With SEC Subpoena After Nasdaq Ouster." Bloomberg News. Retrieved on 24 August 2018 from https://www.bloomberg.com/news/articles/2018-08-01/long-blockchain-gets-hit-with-sec-subpoena-after-nasdaq-ouster.
5. Mohamed, Theron. (9 July 2020). "Chinese tech stock QuantumCTek spikes 924% in trading debut, breaking first-day record." Business Insider. Retrieved on 15 August 2020 from https://markets.businessinsider.com/news/stocks/chinese-tech-stock-quantumctek-soars-record-breaking-924-percent-ipo-2020-7-1029379555#.

Chapter 8

1. Speech by Darryl Willis, VP Oil, Gas, and Energy, Google Cloud at Google. Speech given at D2:Upheaval on 10 October 2018.
2. *Investopedia*. "Moore's Law." Retrieved on 7 November 2018 from https://www.investopedia.com/terms/m/mooreslaw.asp.
3. Gribbin, J. *Computing with Quantum Cats: From Colossus to Qubits*. Prometheus Books: New York. p. 92.
4. Jurvetson, S. (10 December 2016). "Moore's Law Over 120 Years." Flickr. Retrieved on 1 November 2018 from https://www.flickr.com/photos/jurvetson/31409423572/.
5. Speech by Deepu Talla, Vice President and General Manager of Autonomous Machines, NVIDIA, at RoboBusiness on 26 September 2018.
6. Tovey, A (2 April 2014). "When Milliseconds Mean Millions." *The Telegraph*. Retrieved on 12 July 2019 from https://www.telegraph.co.uk/finance/newsbysector/banksandfinance/10736960/High-frequency-trading-when-milliseconds-mean-millions.html.

Chapter 9

1. *FinTech Survey Report* (April 2016). CFA Institute. Retrieved February 11, 2017: https://www.cfainstitute.org/Survey/fintech_survey.PDF.
2. Szmigiera, M. (24 February 2020). "Number of ETFs Worldwide 2003-2019." Statista. Retrieved on 15 August 2020 from www.statista.com/statistics/278249/global-number-of-etfs/.

Chapter 10

1. Farley, A. (2018). "Bearer Bonds: From Popular to Prohibited" Investopedia. Retrieved on 24 August 2018 from https://www.investopedia.com/articles/bonds/08/bearer-bond.asp.
2. Image provided courtesy of Heritage Auctions, HA.com. Retrieved on 24 August 2018 from https://currency.ha.com/itm/miscellaneous/other/-1-000-000-us-treasury-bearer-bond/a/364-15547.s.
3. Lagarde, C (26 April 2018). "Statement by IMF Managing Director Christine Lagarde on Her Participation in the Paris Conference on Terrorism Financing." International Monetary Fund. Retrieved on 24 August 2018 from https://www.imf.org/en/News/Articles/2018/04/26/pr18150-lagarde-on-her-participation-in-the-paris-conference-on-terrorism-financing.
4. "Annual Economics Report." (June 2018). Bank of International Settlements, p. 91-141. Retrieved from https://www.bis.org/publ/arpdf/ar2018e.pdf.
5. Strohm, Chris. (13 August 2020.) "U.S. Says It Seized Cryptocurrency From Three Terrorist Groups." Bloomberg. Retrieved on 15 August 2020 from https://www.bloomberg.com/news/articles/2020-08-13/u-s-says-it-seized-cryptocurrency-from-three-terrorist-groups?sref=GNzrTNIg
6. Powell, J. "Semiannual Monetary Policy Report to the Congress." U.S. Federal Reserve. Retrieved on 12 July 2019 from https://www.federalreserve.gov/newsevents/testimony/powell20190710a.htm.

Chapter 12

1. Delfs, H., Knebl, H. (2015). *Introduction to Cryptography: Principles and Applications.* Third Edition. Springer: New York. P. 343.
2. Ibid. P. 350.
3. Decker, Susan, and Yasiejko, Christopher. (2018). "Forget the Trade War. China Wants to Win Computing Arms Race." Bloomberg.com, Bloomberg, 9 April 2018, www.bloomberg.com/news/articles/2018-04-08/forget-the-trade-war-china-wants-to-win-the-computing-arms-race.
4. US Trade Representative Report. Pp. 10-11. Retrieved on 6 November 2018 from USTR at https://ustr.gov/sites/default/files/Section%20301%20FINAL.PDF.
5. Several of Navarro's books offer insight into US-China policies.
6. "2018 Cost of a Data Breach Study: Global Overview." (July 2018). Ponemon Institute LLC. IBM, p. 13. Retrieved on 25 October 2018 from https://public.dhe.ibm.com/common/ssi/ecm/55/en/55017055usen/2018-global-codb-report_06271811_55017055USEN.pdf.
7. "Internet Security Threat Report." (March 2018). Symantec, Symantec Corporation, p. 9. Retrieved on 25 October 2018 from http://images.mktgassets.symantec.com/Web/Symantec/%7B3a70beb8-c55d-4516-98ed-1d0818a42661%7D_ISTR23_Main-FINAL-APR10.pdf?aid=elq
8. de Wolf, R. (2017). "The Potential Impact of Quantum Computers on Society," p. 2.
9. US Congress. (2019), "Cybersecurity Funding." White House, p. 306. Retrieved on 12 August 2020 from https://www.whitehouse.gov/wp-content/uploads/2019/03/ap_24_cyber_security-fy2020.pdf.
10. "Risk Nexus: Overcome by Cyber Risks? Economic Benefits and Costs of Alternate Cyber Futures." (2015) Atlantic Council, Zurich Insurance Group, p. 11. Retrieved on 25 October 2018 from http://publications.atlanticcouncil.org/cyberrisks/risk-nexus-september-2015-overcome-by-cyber-risks.pdf.

Chapter 14

1. Rodriguez, A. (24 March 2016) "Microsoft's AI millennial chatbot became a racist jerk after less than a day on Twitter." Quartz. Retrieved 17 February 2017: https://qz.com/646825/microsofts-ai-millennial-chatbot-became-a-racist-jerk-after-less-than-a-day-on-twitter/.

Chapter 15

1. U.S. Department of the Treasury. Fiscal Service, Federal Debt: Total Public Debt [GFDEBTN], retrieved from FRED, Federal Reserve Bank of St. Louis; https://fred.stlouisfed.org/series/GFDEBTN, July 21, 2020.
2. Ibid.
3. Federal Reserve Bank of St. Louis and U.S. Office of Management and Budget, Federal Debt: Total Public Debt as Percent of Gross Domestic Product [GFDEGDQ188S], retrieved from FRED, Federal Reserve Bank of St. Louis; https://fred.stlouisfed.org/series/GFDEGDQ188S, July 21, 2020.
4. Gopinath, G. (24 June 2020). IMF Blog: *Reopening from the Great Lockdown: Uneven and Uncertain Recovery*. International Monetary Fund. Retrieved on 20 July 2020 from https://blogs.imf.org/2020/06/24/reopening-from-the-great-lockdown-uneven-and-uncertain-recovery.
5. Ibid.
6. Mayer, J. (18 November 2015). "The Social Security Façade." Retrieved 24 July 2020: https://www.usnews.com/opinion/economic-intelligence/2015/11/18/social-security-and-medicare-have-morphed-into-unsustainable-entitlements.
7. U.S. Social Security Administration. (September 2017). *Fast Facts and Figures About Social Security, 2017*, p. 8. Retrieved on 21 July 2020: https://www.ssa.gov/policy/docs/chartbooks/fast_facts/2017/.
8. U.S. Social Security Administration. (July 2020). *Fast Facts and Figures About Social Security, 2020*, p. 37. Retrieved on 21 July 2020: https://www.ssa.gov/policy/docs/chartbooks/fast_facts/2020/fast_facts20.pdf.
9. Ibid.
10. Ibid.
11. Ibid.
12. World Bank, Population Growth for the United States [SPPOPGROWUSA], retrieved from FRED, Federal Reserve Bank of St. Louis; https://fred.stlouisfed.org/series/SPPOPGROWUSA, June 5, 2018.
13. Last, J. (2013) *What to Expect, When No One's Expecting: America's Coming Demographic Disaster*. New York: Encounter Books, pp. 2-4.
14. Ibid., p. 3.
15. Ibid., p. 109.
16. Coy, Peter. (29 July 2020). "Americans Aren't Making Babies and That's Bad for the Economy." Bloomberg. Retrieved on 15 August 2020 from https://www.bloomberg.com/news/articles/2020-07-29/coronavirus-pandemic-americans-aren-t-making-babies-in-crisis.
17. U.S. Social Security Administration. Retrieved 11 February 2017 from https://www.ssa.gov/history/ratios.html.

Chapter 16

1. Board of Governors of the Federal Reserve System (US), Assets: Total Assets: Total Assets (Less Eliminations from Consolidation): Wednesday Level [WALCL], retrieved from FRED, Federal Reserve Bank of St. Louis; https://fred.stlouisfed.org/series/WALCL, July 21, 2020.
2. European Central Bank, Central Bank Assets for Euro Area (11-19 Countries) [ECBASSETSW], retrieved from FRED, Federal Reserve Bank of St. Louis; https://fred.stlouisfed.org/series/ECBASSETSW, July 21, 2020.
3. Federal Reserve. "The Federal Reserve's Monetary Policy Toolkit: Past, Present, and Future." Retrieved from https://www.federalreserve.gov/newsevents/speech/yellen20160826a.htm.
4. Board of Governors of the Federal Reserve System (US), Effective Federal Funds Rate [FEDFUNDS], retrieved from FRED, Federal Reserve Bank of St. Louis; https://fred.stlouisfed.org/series/FEDFUNDS, July 21, 2020.
5. "Genesis Block." Wikipedia. Bitcoin Wiki. Retrieved on 24 August 2018 from https://en.bitcoin.it/wiki/Main_Page.

Chapter 17

1. Freedman, D. (2016 July/August). "Basic Income: A Sellout of the American Dream." *MIT Technology Review*, p. 52.
2. Ibid., 53.
3. Gentilini, U. (11 January 2017). "Why Universal Basic Income is a Simple, but Effective Idea." World Bank as reprinted by the World Economic Forum. Retrieved 11 February 2017: https://www.weforum.org/agenda/2017/01/in-a-complex-world-the-apparent-simplicity-of-universal-basic-income-is-appealing.
4. Ibid.
5. U.S. Bureau of Labor Statistics, Consumer Price Index for All Urban Consumers: All Items [CPIAUCSL], retrieved on 12 August 2020 from FRED, Federal Reserve Bank of St. Louis; https://fred.stlouisfed.org/series/CPIAUCSL.
6. Moretti, E. (2013). *The New Geography of Jobs.* New York: Mariner Books, p. 13.
7. Kaplan, J. (2015), 184-185.
8. Hamblin, J. (2 February 2017) "How to Make Time Pass Quickly," *The Atlantic*: https://www.theatlantic.com/health/archive/2017/02/how-to-make-time-move/515361/
9. Ibid.
10. Thompson, D. (2015 July/August). "A World Without Work," *The Atlantic*. Retrieved from https://www.theatlantic.com/magazine/archive/2015/07/world-without-work/395294/
11. Image licensed from Adobe Stock.

Chapter 18

1. World Bank. Retrieved on 12 July 2019 from https://globalfindex.worldbank.org/.
2. "2017 FDIC National Survey of Unbanked and Underbanked Households." Federal Deposit Insurance Corporation. Retrieved on 12 July 2019 from https://www.fdic.gov/householdsurvey/. "The Global Findex Database: Measuring Financial Inclusion and the Fintech Revolution." (2017).
3. Ibid.
4. World Bank. Retrieved on 12 July 2019 from https://globalfindex.worldbank.org/.
5. "Fintech: The Experience So Far." (27 June 2019). International Monetary Fund.
6. World Bank. Retrieved on 12 July 2019 from https://globalfindex.worldbank.org/.
7. Ibid.

Chapter 19

1. Welsh, H. (9 November 2018). "Social, Environmental & Sustainable Governance Shareholder Proposals in 2018." *Securities and Exchange Commission*, Sustainable Investments Institute. Retrieved on 12 July 2019 from www.sec.gov/comments/4-725/4725-4636528-176443.pdf.
2. Ibid.
3. "The Activist Investing Annual Review." (2020). *Activist Insight.* Retrieved on 12 August 2020 from https://www.activistinsight.com/research/TheActivistInvesting_AnnualReview_2020.pdf.
4. Ibid.
5. This comes on the heels of pressure from activist investor pushes on the Exxon board for a lack of ESG oversight. "Exxon Board Targeted for Lack of ESG Oversight." (May 11, 2019). National Association of Corporate Directors. Retrieved on 12 July 2019 https://tinyurl.com/NACDExxon2019.

Conclusion

1. Pierron, A. (16 May 2019). "Workforce of the Future: Transplanting Technology Skill Sets to the Capital Markets." Opimas. Retrieved on 13 July 2019 from www.opimas.com/research/472/detail/.
2. "Unemployment rate and earning by educational attainment." (4 September 2019). Employment Projections, U.S. Bureau of Labor Statistics. Retrieved on 24 July 2020 from: https://www.bls.gov/emp/chart-unemployment-earnings-education.htm.

ABOUT THE AUTHOR

Mr. Schenker is the President of Prestige Economics and Chairman of The Futurist Institute. He has been ranked one of the most accurate financial forecasters and futurists in the world. Bloomberg News has ranked Mr. Schenker a top forecaster in 44 categories, including #1 in the world for his accuracy in 25 categories, including for his forecasts of the Euro, the British Pound, the Russian Ruble, the Chinese RMB, crude oil prices, natural gas prices, gold prices, industrial metals prices, agricultural commodity prices, and U.S. jobs.

Mr. Schenker was ranked one of the top 100 most influential financial advisors in the world by Investopedia in 2018. His work has been featured in *The Wall Street Journal, The New York Times,* and the *Frankfurter Allgemeine Zeitung*. He has appeared on CNBC, CNN, ABC, NBC, MSNBC, Fox, Fox Business, BNN, Bloomberg Germany, and the BBC. Mr. Schenker has also been a guest host of Bloomberg Television, and he is a contributor for *Bloomberg Opinion*.

Mr. Schenker attends OPEC and Fed events, and he has given keynotes for private companies, public corporations, industry groups, and the U.S. Federal Reserve. He has advised NATO and the U.S. government on the future of work, blockchain, Bitcoin, cryptocurrency, quantum computing, data analysis, forecasting, and fake news. Mr. Schenker has written 28 books. Twelve have been #1 bestsellers, including: *The Future After COVID, Jobs for Robots, Quantum: Computing Nouveau, Commodity Prices 101, Recession-Proof, Futureproof Supply Chain, Electing Recession, The Future of Finance is Now, The Future of Energy, The Dumpster Fire Election,* and *The Robot and Automation Almanac* for 2018 and 2020. Mr. Schenker also wrote *The Promise of Blockchain, Futureproof Supply Chain, The Fog of Data, Financial Risk Management Fundamentals, Midterm Economics, Spikes: Growth Hacking Leadership, Strategic Cost-Cutting, Strategic Cost-Cutting After COVID*, and *Reading the Economic Tea Leaves*. Mr. Schenker was featured as one of the world's foremost futurists in *After Shock*. His research was included in a June 2020 Pentagon report on global competition after COVID-19.

Mr. Schenker advises executives, industry groups, institutional investors, and central banks as the President of Prestige Economics. He also founded The Futurist Institute, for which he created a rigorous course of study that includes The Future of Work, The Future of Transportation, The Future of Data, The Future of Finance, Futurist Fundamentals, The Future of Energy, The Future of Leadership, The Future of Healthcare, The Future of Quantum Computing, and The Future After COVID. Mr. Schenker is also an instructor for LinkedIn Learning courses on Economic Indicators, Risk Management, Audit and Due Diligence, and Recession-Proof Strategies.

Mr. Schenker holds a Master's in Applied Economics from UNC Greensboro, a Master's in Negotiation, Conflict Resolution, and Peacebuilding from CSU Dominguez Hills, a Master's in Germanic Languages and Literature from UNC Chapel Hill, and a Bachelor's in History and German from The University of Virginia. He also holds a Certificate in FinTech from MIT, a Certificate in Supply Chain Management from MIT, a Certificate in Professional Development from UNC, a Certificate in Negotiation from Harvard Law School, a Certificate in Cybersecurity from Carnegie Mellon, and a Professional Certificate in Strategic Foresight from the University of Houston. Mr. Schenker holds the designations CMT® (Chartered Market Technician), and CFP® (Certified Financial Planner). He is also a Certified Futurist and Long-Term Analyst™ and holds the FLTA™ designation.

Before founding Prestige Economics, Mr. Schenker worked as a Risk Specialist at McKinsey and Company, where he provided content direction to trading, risk, and commodity project teams on six continents. Prior to McKinsey, Mr. Schenker was the Chief Energy and Commodity Economist at Wachovia, which is now Wells Fargo.

Based in Austin, Texas, Mr. Schenker is one of only 100 CEOs on the Texas Business Leadership Council, a non-partisan organization that advises Texas elected leadership at the state and federal level. Mr. Schenker is a Governance Fellow of the National Association of Corporate Directors. He also sits on multiple boards and is the VP of Finance on the Executive Committee of The Texas Lyceum, the preeminent non-partisan leadership group in Texas.

TOP FORECASTER ACCURACY RANKINGS

Prestige Economics has been recognized as the most accurate independent commodity and financial market research firm in the world. As the only forecaster for Prestige Economics, Jason Schenker is very proud that Bloomberg News has ranked him a top forecaster in 44 different categories since 2011, including #1 in the world in 25 different forecast categories.

Mr. Schenker has been top ranked as a forecaster of economic indicators, energy prices, metals prices, agricultural prices, and foreign exchange rates.

ECONOMICS TOP RANKINGS

#1 Non-Farm Payroll Forecaster in the World
#1 New Home Sales Forecaster in the World
#2 U.S. Unemployment Rate Forecaster in the World
#3 Durable Goods Orders Forecaster in the World
#6 Consumer Confidence Forecaster in the World
#7 ISM Manufacturing Index Forecaster in the World
#7 U.S. Housing Starts Forecaster in the World

ENERGY PRICE TOP RANKINGS

#1 WTI Crude Oil Price Forecaster in the World

#1 Brent Crude Oil Price Forecaster in the World

#1 Henry Hub Natural Gas Price Forecaster in the World

METALS PRICE TOP RANKINGS

#1 Gold Price Forecaster in the World

#1 Platinum Price Forecaster in the World

#1 Palladium Price Forecaster in the World

#1 Industrial Metals Price Forecaster in the World

#1 Copper Price Forecaster in the World

#1 Aluminum Price Forecaster in the World

#1 Nickel Price Forecaster in the World

#1 Tin Price Forecaster in the World

#1 Zinc Price Forecaster in the World

#2 Precious Metals Price Forecaster in the World

#2 Silver Price Forecaster in the World

#2 Lead Price Forecaster in the World

#2 Iron Ore Price Forecaster in the World

AGRICULTURAL PRICE TOP RANKINGS

#1 Coffee Price Forecaster in the World

#1 Cotton Price Forecaster in the World

#1 Sugar Price Forecaster in the World

#1 Soybean Price Forecaster in the World

FOREIGN EXCHANGE TOP RANKINGS

#1 Euro Forecaster in the World
#1 British Pound Forecaster in the World
#1 Swiss Franc Forecaster in the World
#1 Chinese RMB Forecaster in the World
#1 Russian Ruble Forecaster in the World
#1 Brazilian Real Forecaster in the World
#2 Turkish Lira Forecaster in the World
#3 Major Currency Forecaster in the World
#3 Canadian Dollar Forecaster in the World
#4 Japanese Yen Forecaster in the World
#5 Australian Dollar Forecaster in the World
#6 Polish Złoty Forecaster in the World
#7 Mexican Peso Forecaster in the World
#1 EURCHF Forecaster in the World
#2 EURJPY Forecaster in the World
#2 EURGBP Forecaster in the World
#2 EURRUB Forecaster in the World

More information about Prestige Economics:

www.prestigeeconomics.com

THE FUTURIST INSTITUTE

FI THE FUTURIST INSTITUTE

The Futurist Institute was founded in 2016 to help analysts, executives, and professionals incorporate technology and trend risks and opportunities into strategic planning. The Futurist Institute confers the Futurist and Long-Term Analyst™ (FLTA) designation and helps analysts become Certified Futurists™. Our courses have been approved for continuing education hours by the Certified Financial Planner Board of Standards (CFP Board).

Current Courses

The Future After COVID
The Future of Work
The Future of Data
The Future of Energy
The Future of Finance
The Future of Healthcare
The Future of Leadership
The Future of Transportation
Futurist Fundamentals
Quantum Computing
Write the Future

Visit The Futurist Institute:

www.futuristinstitute.org

PUBLISHER

Prestige Professional Publishing was founded in 2011 to produce insightful and timely professional reference books. We are registered with the Library of Congress.

Published Titles

Be the Shredder, Not the Shred
Commodity Prices 101
Electing Recession
Financial Risk Management Fundamentals
Futureproof Supply Chain
A Gentle Introduction to Audit and Due Diligence
Jobs for Robots
Midterm Economics
Quantum: Computing Nouveau
Reading the Economic Tea Leaves
Recession-Proof Career Strategies After COVID
Robot-Proof Yourself
Spikes: Growth Hacking Leadership
Strategic Cost-Cutting
Strategic Cost-Cutting After COVID
The Dumpster Fire Election
The Economics of Revolt and Revolution
The Fog of Data
The Future After COVID
The Future of Energy
The Future of Finance After COVID
The Future of Finance is Now

PUBLISHER

Published Titles

The Promise of Blockchain
Write the Future
The Robot and Automation Almanac — 2018
The Robot and Automation Almanac — 2019
The Robot and Automation Almanac — 2020

Forthcoming Titles

Content Monster
Disruption Warfare
The Future of Agriculture
The Future of Healthcare
The Future of Travel and Leisure
The Robot and Automation Almanac — 2021

JOBS FOR ROBOTS

Jobs for Robots provides an in-depth look at the future of automation and robots, with a focus on the opportunities as well as the risks ahead. Job creation in coming years will be extremely strong for the kind of workers that do not require payroll taxes, healthcare, or vacation: robots. *Jobs for Robots* was published in February 2017. This book has been a #1 bestseller on Amazon.

FUTUREPROOF SUPPLY CHAIN

Futureproof Supply Chain examines more than a dozen major risks ahead — and how companies, industries, and individuals can prepare to be futureproof. The book was published in February 2019. This book has been a #1 bestseller on Amazon.

THE FUTURE AFTER COVID

In *The Future After COVID*, top-ranked forecaster and Chairman of The Futurist Institute Jason Schenker offers a futurist perspective into the potential long-term changes, challenges, and opportunities that COVID-19 is likely to have for over a dozen different critical fields and industries. The book was published in April 2020. This book has been an international bestseller.

DISCLAIMER

FROM THE AUTHOR

The following disclaimer applies to any content in this book:

This book is commentary intended for general information use only and is not investment advice. Jason Schenker does not make recommendations on any specific or general investments, investment types, asset classes, non-regulated markets, specific equities, bonds, or other investment vehicles. Jason Schenker does not guarantee the completeness or accuracy of analyses and statements in this book, nor does Jason Schenker assume any liability for any losses that may result from the reliance by any person or entity on this information. Opinions, forecasts, and information are subject to change without notice. This book does not represent a solicitation or offer of financial or advisory services or products; this book is only market commentary intended and written for general information use only. This book does not constitute investment advice. All links were correct and active at the time this book was published.

DISCLAIMER

FROM THE PUBLISHER

The following disclaimer applies to any content in this book:

This book is commentary intended for general information use only and is not investment advice. Prestige Professional Publishing, LLC does not make recommendations on any specific or general investments, investment types, asset classes, non-regulated markets, specific equities, bonds, or other investment vehicles. Prestige Professional Publishing, LLC does not guarantee the completeness or accuracy of analyses and statements in this book, nor does Prestige Professional Publishing, LLC assume any liability for any losses that may result from the reliance by any person or entity on this information. Opinions, forecasts, and information are subject to change without notice. This book does not represent a solicitation or offer of financial or advisory services or products; this book is only market commentary intended and written for general information use only. This book does not constitute investment advice. All links were correct and active at the time this book was published.

Prestige Professional Publishing, LLC

4412 City Park Road #4

Austin, Texas 78730

www.prestigeprofessionalpublishing.com

ISBN: 978-1-946197-99-3 *Paperback*

978-1-946197-65-8 *Ebook*